Hiking the North Shore

Other titles in the series:

Camping the North Shore, 2nd edition: A guide to the best campgrounds in Minnesota's spectacular Lake Superior region

Skiing the North Shore: A guide to cross country trails in Minnesota's spectacular Lake Superior region

Hiking the North Shore

50 fabulous day hikes in Minnesota's
spectacular Lake Superior region

SECOND EDITION

ANDREW SLADE

THERE AND
BACK BOOKS
READ. GO. DISCOVER.

Duluth, Minnesota

Third revised printing (Second Edition), January 2021
Second revised printing (Second Edition), June 2018
First Printing (Second Edition), January 2017
Third revised printing, September 2014
Second revised printing, March 2012
First printing, March 2011

Book designer: Sally Rauschenfels

Editor and proofreader: Gail Trowbridge

Cover photograph © Travis Novitsky, www.travisnovitsky.com
Interior photographs © Andrew Slade unless otherwise noted
Back cover photograph © jimkruger, istockphoto.com

ISBN 978-0-9794675-3-0
Library of Congress Control Number: 2016958701

Printed in the United States of America

There & Back Books, Duluth, Minnesota | bestnorthshore.com

To Walter and Dick,
who taught Sally and me what trails to follow
and where we should blaze our own.

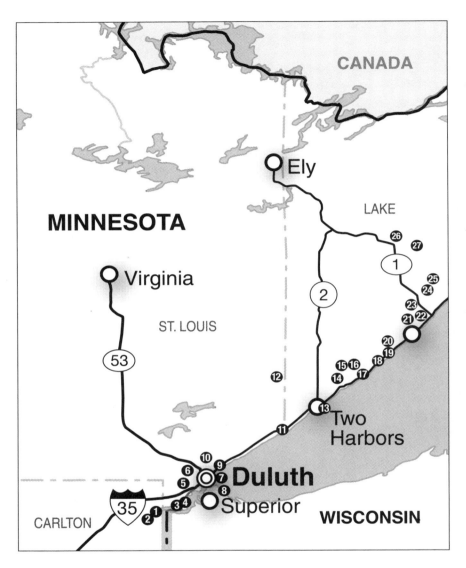

Hiking the North Shore
50 fabulous day hikes in Minnesota's spectacular
Lake Superior region

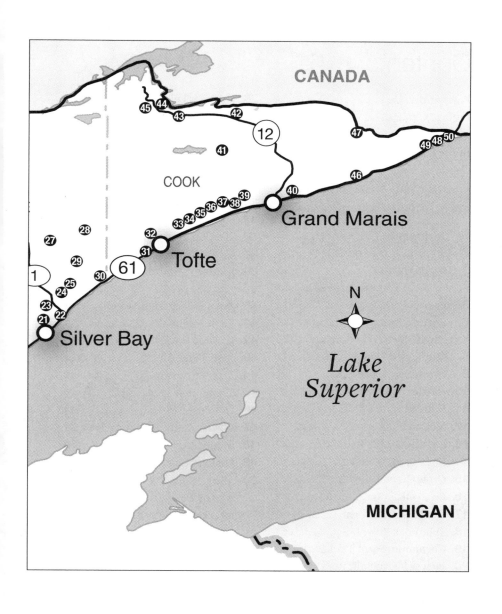

Contents

Hiking the North Shore: 50 fabulous day hikes

Foreword

For years, we have hiked the trails of the Minnesota North Shore for pleasure and inspiration. We have led groups, explored in all seasons and developed a love that can only come from the real intimacy of placing one foot in front of the other and pausing to see the designs in the rocks, plants and landscape. We have explored the parks and the backpack trails, walked the Gitchi Gami bike trail, and enjoyed the loops that connect the various resorts.

When Andrew asked us to review this book and make comments, Mike thought, "This will be easy, I'm sure I have walked all the trails that are in the book and I can just say, 'Good job, Andrew'." We are the old "coots" and Andrew was once one of Mike's college students, so what could he show us? Sure he was practically born on a North Shore waterfall, and yes he cut his baby teeth on icicles hanging from stone arches, but he is a young guy with lots of things to occupy his mind and time.

We thought this would be a book of reminiscences. And it was. In September 2010 we completed a 1,550-mile walk around Lake Superior. Andrew was with us on the first day walking down Minnesota Point and on the last when we returned to Duluth. (Thanks, Andrew, for including a note and photos on page 31 and 35 about our walk.)

But it's not just a book of reminiscences. In reviewing this new book we found new places to explore. Andrew did it. He was so thorough that even the most dedicated of North Shore trekkers will find new trails to occupy future years of wandering. And Kate is anxious to try the Spirit Mountain Alpine Coaster!

Like an unexpected gift under the Christmas tree, here are 50 trails waiting for our feet. Andrew really explored this landscape and we really appreciate it. Just open up the book randomly and put your finger on a page and you have the guide to adventure and discovery. Like a true naturalist Andrew was inspired by all that he saw, whether a new bird, a new flower, wolf scat, a quirky mushroom, or the view from a rocky overlook. With your eyes wide open, there was no such thing as a boring walk.

During our walk around the lake, we depended on local knowledge to help us find our way. People were very kind and anxious to help, but we discovered that many of them only had a rough idea of what the shoreline or trail might be like. They had obviously not walked it for some time, if at all. You don't have to worry about that when you use this guide. Andrew has ground truthed each and every trail. We once wrote a book about hiking trails and we know the dedication and effort it takes to "walk the talk." But it is the only way to ensure quality and truth in advertising.

Equally important is the accurate inclusion of distance. On our walk around Lake Superior, distances became a sore point. Mike had done his best to figure out the exact mileage of each day's hike, but using a string to measure the distance on a small map of the lake meant there would be some disparity, and after 15 miles, an unexpected extra mile feels interminable. All the hikes in this book have their mileage listed, are less than 12 miles long, and most importantly, indicate whether there are steep portions or not—another critical factor for the enjoyment of some.

The black and white photos throughout the book show a nice mix of people, places, and natural features, but the ones we liked best were those with the photogenic, cuddly Miss Chloe in them. We know the pleasure of walking with your dog, possibly the best hiking companion around. They are continually in a state of thrall and never complain about the distance, which Mike can most appreciate. The periodic entry called "Eats, Treats and Lodging" is another bonus in this guidebook, because there is nothing better, in Kate's opinion, than a visit to a local eatery or lodging at the end of a pleasant and sometimes challenging hike. It is the cherry on top of the already delicious day.

Andrew Slade is quickly becoming the voice of the Minnesota shore of Lake Superior and having covered the entire shore, we only wish there could be such a great voice in every state and province.

Get out on the trail and see for yourself.

— **Mike Link and Kate Crowley,** facebook.com/fullcirclesuperior

Mike Link and Kate Crowley hiked the Lake Superior shoreline for over 1,500 miles, including the rocky shore of Cascade River State Park.

Preface

"Climb the mountains and get their good tidings. Nature's peace will flow into you as sunshine flows into trees. The winds will blow their own freshness into you, and the storms their energy, while cares will drop off like autumn leaves."

— John Muir

I wrote this book to save the world. I believe that the more time you spend hiking, the more you care about the environment you're in. And the more you care, the more you'll choose to take care of it.

I've been hiking the North Shore since I was a kid. My extended family would drive out on the back roads above Highway 61 to a river bridge. My father and uncles would lead us on fishermen's trails miles and miles back down the river to Lake Superior. I first climbed Eagle Mountain when I was ten or twelve, followed by an unplanned continuation of the hike all the way to Brule Lake. Ten years before the Superior Hiking Trail made it easy, my father and I tried to hike up Carlton Peak but could not find a trail.

Through these adventures, I gained comfort with, and perspective on, this wild country.

Hiking the North Shore describes 50 great North Shore day hikes. The hikes are found from Duluth to Grand Portage, and along inland roads like Highway 1, the Cramer Road and the Gunflint Trail. Each hike has detailed directions to the trailhead, overview information like distance and time, and a great map.

I've hiked every trail in this book, often more than once. Between April 2008 and November 2009, I hiked at least 300 miles in what I called "total dork mode." If you saw the guy with the GPS unit swinging from his neck, a camera in one hand and a steno notebook in the other, that was me.

I wasn't a very good hike partner, as I had to stop every hundred feet or so to write in my book or take pictures. The one who tolerated me best was my standard poodle Chloe, who came along on almost half the hikes. She went crazy at the mere mention of a car ride, thinking just maybe it would be another trail adventure. Without her, many of the photos in this book would be empty of anything but the scenery.

After nearly every hiking day I'd finish up with a hot drink or an ice cream treat and reflect on the day's adventures. Sitting there at the Grand Marais Dairy Queen or the Coho Café in Tofte, I'd ask myself or my hiking companion, "Why would someone else want to do that hike?" I hope this book answers that question for you. Get out there, enjoy these woods, these beautiful rivers and lakes. Maybe you'll want to help take care of them, too.

Not every hike I took made it into the book. I tried for months to describe Duluth's Chester Bowl trails. While the differences between walking, skiing and hiking trails are obvious to the locals, they're impossible to describe to someone new. In another case, I was high atop an incredibly scenic bluff on the Border Route Trail, and I ran into a rare plant ecologist. He politely asked me not to direct any more foot traffic toward the endangered flora at this site.

My sons came along on about ten hikes. I tried to coax them one summer with hints of some fancy electronic gadget if they finished all the state park hiking club trails. They lost interest after finding the third password on a hot July day.

There were a few lovely days hiking with my beautiful wife Sally, with one especially great day at LeVeaux and Oberg mountains.

In the terrific North Shore state parks, the following staff were extremely helpful: Kate Flitsch, Cascade River State Park; Kris Hiller, Jay Cooke State Park; Paul Sundberg, Gooseberry Falls State Park; Lisa Angelos, Split Rock Lighthouse State Park; Gary Hoeft and Jim Bischoff, Tettegouche, George H. Crosby and Temperance River state parks; and Travis Novitsky, Grand Portage State Park.

Gayle Coyer of the Superior Hiking Trail Association answered one oddball question after another. Ed Solstad is the voice and conscience of the Border Route Trail. Rod McKenzie of the McKenzie map company was very generous in sharing copies of their fine maps. The reference staff at the Duluth Public Library helped me find and use their extensive resources.

Mike Link and Kate Crowley wrote the foreword for the book and inspired hikers from all around the region. They are also fine hiking companions.

These trails are maintained by hundreds of loyal volunteers and trail workers who could never be thanked enough.

Thank you, Gail Trowbridge, for helping this book find its voice.

Special thanks to all those folks who tolerated my total geek approach to hiking and came along on the hikes: Sally Rauschenfels, Hans Slade, Noah Slade, Richard Slade, and Albert Wouters. It is Sally who did all the hard work on this book: planning, layout, design and editing. I'm really glad she got away from her office a few times to join me for the fun part.

The best hiking in Minnesota

Minnesota's best hiking is found on the North Shore of Lake Superior. Sure, there are nice trails here and there throughout the land of 10,000 lakes. But for the greatest number of high-quality trails all in one general area, no place is better than the North Shore.

Want proof? Come see for yourself. Here's what you'll find:

Eight beautiful state parks. Ranging from little Grand Portage to big Jay Cooke, all North Shore state parks have at least one terrific hike, and most have multiple day hike options. The parks have preserved some of the most beautiful shoreline, waterfalls and natural ecosystems on the North Shore. Seventeen of the 50 hikes in this book are in state parks.

The Superior National Forest. This huge stretch of public land is best known for canoeing in the Boundary Waters Canoe Area wilderness. There are many miles of well-maintained hiking trails as well. Eighteen of the 50 hikes in this book run through the Superior National Forest, including two that travel into the BWCA.

The Superior Hiking Trail. Consistently rated as one of the top ten long-distance trails in the country, the Superior Hiking Trail is perfect for day hikes as well as overnight backpacking. Volunteers and employees maintain the trails for a consistently excellent hiking experience. Twenty-seven of the 50 hikes in this book are partly or entirely on the Superior Hiking Trail.

In addition, you'll find cities such as Duluth and Two Harbors maintaining trails. There are small volunteer groups building and protecting big wilderness trails like the Kekekabic Trail and the Border Route Trail. One of the best-maintained trails in this book is the Historic Grand Portage, cared for by the National Park Service.

Along the way are some surprises. Where's the longest stretch of Minnesota trail right on the Lake Superior shore? It's in downtown Duluth, on the Lakewalk. Do you have to always hike from one trailhead to another on the Superior Hiking Trail? No, many sections of the SHT have great round-trip destinations like scenic overlooks or waterfalls.

Hiking seasons

Hiking is a four-season activity on the North Shore.

Spring. The snow has typically melted off North Shore trails sometime between early April and early May. May 1 to mid-June is a lovely time for hiking. The waterfalls are running high, wildflowers cover the forest floor, and songs from migrating birds fill the air. Trails can be muddy, so be prepared to get dirty. I like to wear gaiters. The only real insect pests are ticks.

Summer. The best summer hiking is right along the North Shore, at trails like Shovel Point in Tettegouche State Park or Minnesota Point near downtown Duluth. Cool breezes off the lake drive away summer's heat as well as the biting flies found inland. If you're hiking on an inland trail, go early in the day and plan to spend your afternoons in the shade back at your tent, cabin or hotel room.

Fall. Fall is the prime season for North Shore hiking. The trails are generally dry and well-groomed. After mid-August, the bugs are gone. Maple trees come ablaze in middle to late September, and the aspen trees along Highway 61 are alight with color until mid-October. In late fall, the leaves are gone from the trees and the views open up on trails such as the Historic Grand Portage and Silver Creek trails.

Winter. Winter hiking on the North Shore can range from a trek with snowshoes on the Superior Hiking Trail to a scenic walk on frozen but snowless state park trails. The City of Duluth even plows the Lakewalk for winter use. For winter hiking, you might want a trekking pole and a set of lightweight crampons such as Yak Trax. State Park trails are the best bet for the beginning snowshoer, especially since many of the parks rent snowshoes.

What to bring: Plan for safety

Even the shortest hike in a state park can turn into an epic adventure with one wrong turn or the twist of an ankle. Be prepared with the Ten Essentials, first described by The Mountaineers in the 1930s: map, compass, sunglasses and sunscreen, extra food, water and a way to purify it, extra clothes, flashlight, first aid kit, fire starter or matches, and knife.

Many hikers bring a cellphone along for safety. However, cellphone coverage is spotty on the North Shore, especially in the valleys behind the first ridgeline. In an emergency, don't count on using a cellphone. Ironically, you might get five bars on top of remote Eagle Mountain.

In June, July and even in August, mosquitoes and blackflies can make you run, not hike, straight out of the woods—making insect repellent essential. In May, be aware of ticks. You can tuck your pant legs into your socks to prevent picking up ticks along the trail.

Some of the hikes in this book require a state park vehicle permit or a day-use permit for the BWCA. If a permit is needed, that's noted right in the first page of the description.

How to use this book

The goal of this book is to help you find the perfect hike for you and your companions. In many cases, you can leave the guidebook in the car and follow the local signs and maps.

Each trail has a brief summary called **What makes this trail unique,** which highlights special or unusual features found on a particular route. Whether you're outside Grand Marais or in downtown Duluth, there's a good North Shore hike for you within a short drive.

How to find the trailhead gives you driving directions to the trailhead. Directions are typically given from Interstate 35 or from Minnesota Highway 61 and often reference mile markers. The mile markers run from zero in Duluth to 150 in Grand Portage. Mile markers are given in decimals, for example "35.3." Use your odometer to measure the three-tenths of a mile past the mile marker.

The actual hike descriptions are a summary to help you choose and prepare. For most of these hikes, you should be able to leave the book in your car and follow signs and maps along the trail.

Length. The length for hikes are given in miles, and reflect the entire hike. If it's two miles in to a lake and two miles back out again on the same trail, that's a four-mile hike. These are based on my own GPS recordings and occasionally differ from other books and maps.

Time is a range based on the author's experience. Trail runners will do it faster. Backpackers and young families may take longer. A steep two-mile hike up Mt. Josephine will take nearly as long as a four-mile stroll on Duluth's Downtown Lakewalk.

Difficulty is based on length, terrain, and route finding. Easy hikes range from one to three miles and are relatively flat and easy to follow. Moderate hikes range from two to eight miles, have more hills and may require some navigation. Difficult hikes range from three to twelve miles, have steep climbs, go through remote terrain and may be difficult to navigate.

More Info provides essential contact information for the trail, including the organization that maintains the trail. It also mentions recommended maps.

GPS coordinates are for the trailhead only and are meant to help drivers with navigation systems find the parking area for the trail.

Trailhead facilities describes the amenities available at the trailhead, to help you plan for needs such as drinking water, picnicking, and restrooms.

Other options for this hike covers simple ways to extend or shorten the hike as described.

Complete your North Shore hiking experience with **Nearby Eats, Treats and Lodging.** There you'll read about fun, tasty or convenient things to do after your hike.

Join the State Park Hiking Club

Get to know the state parks of the North Shore up close and personal...by joining the club!

Each Minnesota State Park has a designated trail for the Hiking Club. These trails are easy to find and easy to navigate and take you to some of the best parts of the park. On the North Shore, these trails

take you to amazing overlooks, secret waterfalls and lovely forests.

Stop at any park office to purchase your Hiking Club member packet. It includes a club handbook, a statewide map of the parks, and a small fanny pack.

Each Hiking Club Trail has a secret password sign somewhere along the route. Record the password in your club handbook. Add up the mileage of each Hiking Club trail you complete. Once you've reached landmarks like 25 or 100 miles, bring your club handbook to a park office and claim your perk, such as patches or plaques. Hiking all the North Shore state park trails nearly gets you your first 25 mile patch!

Andrew's picks

These trails are all great...for different reasons. Whether you're looking for a daylong challenge or a short stroll with a grandchild, you'll find it on the North Shore. Here are a few of my personal picks and recommendations.

Following the footsteps of history
Historians and interpreters will get a kick out of these:
- St. Louis River Loop, Jay Cooke State Park (Hike #2)
- Enger Tower, Duluth (Hike #6)
- Downtown Lakewalk, Duluth (Hike #9)
- Divide Lake, Isabella (Hike #27)
- Eagle Mountain, Lutsen (Hike #41)
- Centennial Trail, Gunflint Trail (Hike #45)
- Historic Grand Portage, Grand Portage (Hike #49)

Hikes for the naturalist
Watch for birds and buds:
- Western Waterfront Trail, Duluth (Hike #4)
- Duluth Beach Walk, Duluth (Hike #7)
- Leveaux Mountain, Tofte (Hike #33)
- Magnetic Rock Trail, Gunflint Trail (Hike #44)

Psst! Secret password
Learn more than the password on the state park Hiking Club Trails:
- Silver Creek Trail, Jay Cooke State Park (Hike #1)
- Gitchi Gummi Trail, Gooseberry Falls State Park (Hike #17)
- Corundum Point Trail, Split Rock Lighthouse State Park (Hike #19)
- Shovel Point, Tettegouche State Park (Hike #22)

- Humpback Trail, George H. Crosby Manitou State Park (Hike #29)
- Temperance River, Temperance River State Park (Hike #31)
- Lookout Mountain, Cascade River State Park (Hike #38)
- Devil's Kettle, Judge C.R. Magney State Park (Hike #46)
- Middle Falls Trail, Grand Portage State Park (Hike #50)

Safe hikes in deer season

During the two-week deer hunting season, these trails are safe:
- Brewer Park Loop, Duluth (Hike #5)
- Duluth Beach Walk, Duluth (Hike #7)
- Corundum Point, Split Rock Lighthouse State Park (Hike #19)
- Shovel Point, Tettegouche State Park (Hike #22)

Down the M&M Trail

Create young hikers here:
- Crow Creek Valley, Two Harbors (Hike #15)
- Eighteen Lake, Isabella (Hike #26)
- Oberg Mountain, Tofte (Hike #34)
- Magnetic Rock Trail, Gunflint Trail (Hike #44)

Trails that lead to torrents

In a land of waterfalls, these are the best:
- Five Falls Loop, Gooseberry Falls State Park (Hike #16)
- Split Rock River Loop, Split Rock Lighthouse State Park (Hike #18)
- Caribou Falls, Little Marais (Hike #30)
- Temperance River, Temperance River State Park (Hike #31)
- Cascade River Loop, Cascade River State Park (Hike #39)
- Devil's Kettle, Judge C.R. Magney State Park (Hike #46)
- Middle Falls Trail, Grand Portage State Park (Hike #50)

Autumnal adventures

For the reds and oranges of sugar maples in fall, check out:
- Elys Peak, Duluth (Hike #3)
- McCarthy Creek, Two Harbors (Hike #12)
- Section 13, Little Marais (Hike #25)
- Leveaux Mountain, Tofte (Hike #33)
- Oberg Mountain, Tofte (Hike #34)
- Lutsen Gondola Hike, Lutsen (Hike #35)

For the young and the restless

Here's where teenagers can add some adventure to the family hike:

- Lighthouse Point, Two Harbors (Hike #13)
- Gitchi Gummi Trail, Gooseberry Falls State Park (Hike #17)
- Lutsen Gondola Hike, Lutsen (Hike #35)

Gut busters

Not the longest, these are the toughest:
- Encampment River, Two Harbors (Hike #14)
- Wolf Ridge Fantasia, Little Marais (Hike #24)
- Mt. Josephine, Grand Portage (Hike #48)

Daylong challenges

Pack a lunch...and dinner...for these long, hard hikes:
- Beaver Bay to Split Rock, Beaver Bay (Hike #20)
- Tettegouche Lakes Loop, Tettegouche State Park (Hike #23)
- Caribou Trail to Cascade (Hike #37)
- Caribou Rock Trail, Gunflint Trail (Hike #42)

Walk in winter

Strap on the snowshoes for these hikes:
- Hartley Nature Center, Duluth (rentals in Center) (Hike #10)
- Gitchi Gummi Trail, Gooseberry Falls State Park (Hike #17)
- Leveaux Mountain, Tofte (rentals in town) (Hike #33)
- Carlton Peak, Tofte (rentals in town) (Hike #32)
- Middle Falls Trail, Grand Portage State Park (rentals in park) (Hike #50)

Best scenery—inland views

For dramatic views of rugged terrain, check out:
- Elys Peak, Duluth (Hike #3)
- Twin Lakes Trail, Silver Bay (Hike #21)
- Section 13, Little Marais (Hike #25)
- Caribou Trail to Lutsen, Lutsen (Hike #36)
- Caribou Trail to Cascade River, Lutsen (Hike #37)
- Eagle Mountain, Lutsen (Hike #41)
- Border Route Sampler, Hovland (Hike #47)

Best scenery—Lake Superior views

If you want a big view of the Big Lake, head here:
- Lighthouse Point, Two Harbors (Hike #13)
- Shovel Point, Tettegouche State Park (Hike #22)
- Carlton Peak, Tofte (Hike #32)
- Oberg Mountain, Tofte (Hike #34)

- Devil Track to Pincushion, Grand Marais (Hike #40)
- Mount Josephine, Grand Portage (Hike #48)

If you like a crowd

Some days, it's nice to have some company. You'll find it on these trails:
- Downtown Lakewalk, Duluth (Hike #9)
- Lighthouse Point, Two Harbors (Hike #13)
- Five Falls Loop, Gooseberry Falls State Park (Hike #16)
- Split Rock River Loop, Split Rock Lighthouse State Park (Hike #18)
- Shovel Point, Tettegouche State Park (Hike #22)
- Oberg Mountain, Tofte (Hike #34)

When you want to be alone

Head far off the beaten path for these trails :
- Divide Lake, Isabella (Hike #27)
- Caribou Rock Trail, Gunflint Trail (Hike #42)
- Border Route Sampler, Hovland (Hike #47)

Trail runners' favorites

Andy Holak of Duluth's Adventure Running Company recommends these trails:
- Elys Peak, Duluth (Hike #3)
- Brewer Park Loop, Duluth (Hike #5)
- Twin Lakes Trail, Silver Bay (Hike #21)
- Oberg Mountain, Tofte (Hike #34)
- Mt. Josephine Trail, Grand Portage (Hike #48)

If you want to backpack

These trails have the best backcountry campsites:
- Split Rock River Loop, Split Rock Lighthouse State Park (Hike #18)
- Corundum Point Trail, Split Rock Lighthouse State Park (Hike #19)
- Divide Lake, Isabella (Hike #27)
- Hogback Lake, Finland (Hike #28)
- Eagle Mountain, Lutsen (Hike #41)
- Cascade River Loop, Cascade River State Park (Hike #39)
- Devil Track to Pincushion, Grand Marais (Hike #40)

01 Silver Creek Trail

A 3.6 mile loop in Jay Cooke State Park near Carlton

State Park
Hiking
Club
TRAIL

The St. Louis River carves a dramatic gorge along the River Trail, and can be accessed by hikers on the Silver Creek Trail.

▶ **What makes it unique.** In early summer, you can see a huge colony of yellow ladyslippers. In fall, the hardwood forest burns with colors from top to bottom.

▶ **Finding the trailhead.** Drive three miles east of Carlton on Highway 210 to the River Inn Visitor Center.

▶ **A State Park vehicle permit is required.**

This is a nature lover's loop through mostly deciduous forests. Once you've crossed the famous swinging bridge over the St. Louis River, there are few big landscape views. Instead, you can experience a variety of forest habitats, from sugar maple and basswood trees to spruce trees. The display of yellow lady's slippers along this trail in May and June is remarkable.

The Silver Creek Trail is Jay Cooke State Park's official Hiking Club Trail. Stop at the park office to sign up for the Club, and keep your eye out for the password along the trail. Signage for the Hiking Club Trail route is generally

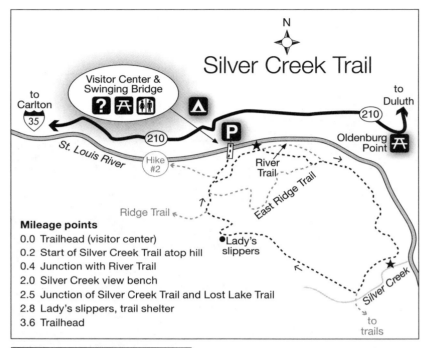

Silver Creek Trail

Visitor Center & Swinging Bridge

to Carlton
35

210

to Duluth
210

St. Louis River

Hike #2

P

Oldenburg Point

River Trail

East Ridge Trail

Ridge Trail

Silver Creek

Mileage points
0.0 Trailhead (visitor center)
0.2 Start of Silver Creek Trail atop hill
0.4 Junction with River Trail
2.0 Silver Creek view bench
2.5 Junction of Silver Creek Trail and Lost Lake Trail
2.8 Lady's slippers, trail shelter
3.6 Trailhead

Lady's slippers

to trails

Distance: 3.6 miles

Time: 1.5 to 2.5 hours

Difficulty: moderate
Springtime mud and rolling hills can make this a challenging trek for young children.

More info:
Jay Cooke State Park
www.dnr.state.mn.us/state_parks/jay_cooke
(218) 673-7000
Map available at Visitor Center.

GPS coordinates:
N 46° 39.28'
W 092° 22.24'

Trailhead facilities: Restrooms, campground, drinking water, visitor information, and vending machines.

excellent, with directional signs at each intersection starting at the swinging bridge.

The trail is wide and is used for XC skiing in the winter. As is often the case, that means there is no one treadway to follow, just a swath of grass. In the spring, the trail can be quite muddy, sometimes even with standing water. In the late summer and during fall colors, the trail offers premium hiking.

From the parking lot, you'll cross the swinging bridge, then head up the hill, following signs for the Hiking Club Trail the whole way. If you'd rather explore the river bank and its fascinating rocks, you can take River Trail, which begins off the Silver Creek Trail 0.4 miles in at a scenic bench. You won't miss the Hiking Club password if you do this.

Be sure to stop at the halfway point of the loop. At an overlook of pretty little Silver Creek, you'll find a bench and a log trail shelter.

The southern half of the loop is drier and more varied than the northern half. Perhaps because it is largely south-facing, the trail is more open and has more drought-tolerant conifer trees. If what you most desire is to see the lady's slippers, take this route in reverse. There is a pleasant trail shelter about 70 yards south of the lady's slippers. A round-trip hike to the flowers and the shelter is about 1.5 miles. This part of the route goes through many intersections, so follow your map carefully.

Nearby Eats, Treats & Lodging

Camping in Jay Cooke State Park makes for a great adventure vacation, with the Willard Munger bike trail and scenic exploration all nearby. The campground is featured in *Camping the North Shore,* by Andrew Slade.

❱ **Other options for this hike.** Jay Cooke State Park is full of hiking trails, although most of them are also XC ski trails in winter and might share the grass and mud conditions of this loop during the spring season. There are four backcountry campsites near this loop, providing a challenge for the beginning backpacker.

Yellow lady's slipper is found in huge colonies along this trail, near the trail shelter about 300 yards south of the Ridge Trail junction.

Explore Jay Cooke State Park

Part historical treasure, part naturalist's delight, Jay Cooke is a diverse and expansive state park on the edge of urban Duluth, Minnesota. Within you'll find nearly 8,000 acres and 50 miles of hiking trails (twice as many as Tettegouche State Park). The park surrounds a dramatic gorge of the St. Louis River, the largest American tributary to Lake Superior.

Jay Cooke was severely damaged in the floods of June 2012. The iconic swinging bridge was swept off its pilings and didn't reopen for a year. The dike holding back Forbay Lake burst, sending a wall of water that cut the park in two. Entire segments of hiking trails slid away with the heavy rains, and swollen creeks washed out footbridges. Most of the major repairs have been done, but scars from the flood are everywhere,

Adventurous hikers can set up camp at the main state park campground, which has unique camper cabins for those without a tent or RV. Trails leave right from the campground, including hiking trails and a spur to the paved Munger bike trail.

Historic highlights include the 1906 Thomson hydroelectric plant, the Thomson pioneer cemetery and the Grand Portage of the St. Louis River, parts of which can still be hiked today.

02 St. Louis River Loop

A 5.5 mile loop hike in Jay Cooke State Park near Carlton

The swinging bridge carries hikers safely across the St. Louis River to explore the undeveloped southern side of Jay Cooke State Park, including the River Loop hike.

▶ **What makes it unique.** Get up close and personal with the mighty St. Louis River as it runs through the heart of Jay Cooke State Park.

▶ **Finding the trailhead.** Follow signs from Interstate 35 exit to Carlton—17 miles south of Duluth. From Carlton travel 3 miles east on Highway 210 to the Jay Cooke State Park River Inn Visitor Center.

▶ **A State Park vehicle permit is required.**

This long loop takes you up the far side of the St. Louis River along narrow hiking trails, then returns you to the visitor center along biking, hiking, and XC ski trails. You'll cross the St. Louis River twice, first on the famous swinging bridge, then on an old railroad bridge.

You'll hike the following trails, listed in order: Carlton Trail, the Munger Trail, the Thomson Trail, the Thomson Loop XC ski trail and the CCC Trail.

From the visitor center area, find your way to the swinging bridge, which you'll cross. Head straight up the hill on the main wide trail, but keep an eye out for the "Carlton Trail," which leaves this main trail about three quarters of

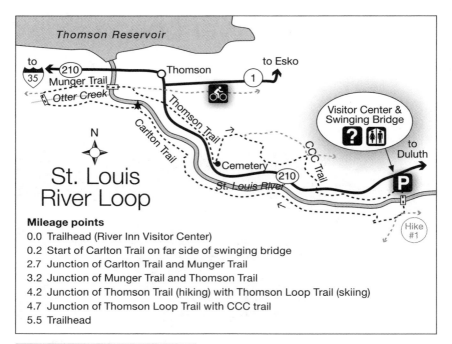

St. Louis River Loop

Mileage points
0.0 Trailhead (River Inn Visitor Center)
0.2 Start of Carlton Trail on far side of swinging bridge
2.7 Junction of Carlton Trail and Munger Trail
3.2 Junction of Munger Trail and Thomson Trail
4.2 Junction of Thomson Trail (hiking) with Thomson Loop Trail (skiing)
4.7 Junction of Thomson Loop Trail with CCC trail
5.5 Trailhead

Distance: 5.5 miles

Time: 2 to 3 hours

Difficulty: moderate. From tricky footing on the south side of the St. Louis River to tricky navigating on the north side, this trail keeps you paying attention.

More info:
Jay Cooke State Park
www.dnr.state.mn.us/state_parks/jay_cooke (218) 673-7000
Map available at Visitor Center

GPS coordinates:
46° 39.28'
92° 22.24'

Trailhead facilities: Restrooms, campground, drinking water, visitor information, and vending machines.

the way up the hill. This is a true hiking trail, one that's narrow and winding and climbs up and down the clay banks of the river valley.

Side trails and connector trails reach out primarily to the left, but stay with the river on your right. The forest changes from northern hardwood trees such as sugar maple and basswood, to paper birch trees, to white pine trees. A side trail about 45 minutes in takes you to a pleasant waterfall and a massive white pine tree, perfect for a snack break.

You'll also enjoy a big view of the river gorge from a rocky ridge traverse. Watch for the railroad bridge in the gorge below; you'll be crossing that bridge in about one mile.

A massive white pine stands watch over a short waterfall along the south bank of the St. Louis River.

Find headstones from the 1800s at the Thomson pioneer cemetery.

After a pretty stretch along Otter Creek, the Carlton Trail reaches the Munger Trail, a paved multipurpose trail. Go right on the Munger Trail and cross the St. Louis River on the old, high railroad bridge. This bridge is a popular rest area, with rapids below.

The second half of the loop follows a few different trails through interesting terrain. The Thomson Trail turns off the Munger Trail about 200 yards past the bridge. Follow the Thomson Trail as it crosses Highway 210, briefly goes through the cut for the old Lake Superior and Mississippi Railroad along Highway 210, and finally heads up into the Thomson pioneer cemetery. The cemetery markers are weatherbeaten, falling over and scattered, but you can still pick out some of the pioneer names and dates.

Past the cemetery, you'll meet the Thomson Loop XC ski trail, a wide and grassy trail. Turn right at the CCC trail. The CCC trail crosses Highway 210 again on its way down to the St. Louis River and big white pine trees. Within a few minutes of walking along the river bank, you're back to the River Inn Visitor Center and your car.

03 Elys Peak

A 6.6 mile out-and-back hike on the Superior Hiking Trail in Duluth

Elys Peak rises from the St. Louis River valley in the wilds of western Duluth.

▶ What makes it unique. With dramatic views of the St. Louis River valley and a climb to a rugged stony peak, this is the closest thing on the North Shore to a Rocky Mountain timberline hike.

▶ Finding the trailhead. Take Interstate 35 to Boundary Ave. exit. Go south towards Spirit Mountain Recreation Area; Boundary Ave. turns into Skyline Parkway. You'll turn left at the stop sign at the junction with Mountain Drive. Drive 2.3 miles total on Skyline Parkway. Parking lot is on left side of the road; there are signs both for the Superior Hiking Trail and for the Magney XC ski trails.

There are two peaks along this route: Bardon and Elys. It is Elys Peak you'll remember, with its dramatic stony summit and 360-degree view. Along the way to the summit you'll pass through a beautiful deciduous forest, including the unique Magney Natural Area. In the spring, the forest floor is awash with spring wildflowers. In the fall, dramatic colors make the hike beautiful.

From the Magney parking lot, the trail runs quickly downhill to cross Snively Creek, followed by a gradual climb back up to Skyline Parkway. Remember this

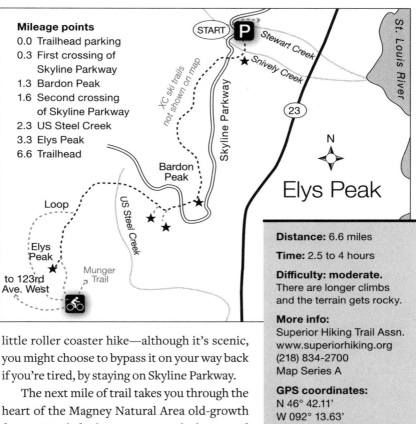

Mileage points
0.0 Trailhead parking
0.3 First crossing of
    Skyline Parkway
1.3 Bardon Peak
1.6 Second crossing
    of Skyline Parkway
2.3 US Steel Creek
3.3 Elys Peak
6.6 Trailhead

START 🅿 Stewart Creek
Snively Creek
XC ski trails not shown on map
Skyline Parkway
23

Bardon Peak

St. Louis River

N

Elys Peak

Loop
US Steel Creek
Elys Peak
to 123rd Ave. West
Munger Trail

Distance: 6.6 miles

Time: 2.5 to 4 hours

Difficulty: moderate.
There are longer climbs
and the terrain gets rocky.

More info:
Superior Hiking Trail Assn.
www.superiorhiking.org
(218) 834-2700
Map Series A

GPS coordinates:
N 46° 42.11'
W 092° 13.63'

Trailhead facilities: None

little roller coaster hike—although it's scenic,
you might choose to bypass it on your way back
if you're tired, by staying on Skyline Parkway.

The next mile of trail takes you through the
heart of the Magney Natural Area old-growth
forest. Watch for large sugar maple, basswood
and ironwood trees. (You can tell from their
growth patterns and all the dead trees on the
ground that this is old-growth forest.) Before leaf-out happens in May, flowers
such as spring beauty, trillium, anemone and bellwort bloom profusely. The trail
crosses the Magney XC ski trail twice.

Bardon Peak does not have a dramatic summit, just a rocky ridgeline with
stunted trees and four overlooks of Morgan Park. At one overlook, you can see
180 degrees—from Enger Tower on the left to the Oliver Bridge across the St.
Louis River on the right. The Bardon family, for whom the peak is named, settled
in both Superior and western Duluth.

The trail recrosses Skyline Parkway. Right after that crossing, there are
two spurs to overlook trails; the first is the more interesting. The trail cuts

through more northern hardwood forest, crosses the US Steel Creek, then emerges onto open rocky fields. In August, these rocky fields can be full of blueberries.

This is fun hiking. Blue-studded posts lead the way through open patches of rocky and mossy field as the trail approaches the very visible Elys Peak ahead. An SHT loop trail enters from the right. The short ascent to the summit is actually a spur off the Superior Hiking Trail and this junction can be hard to spot, so look for white blazes underfoot going up the rocky slope. At the summit, enjoy a 360-degree view including distant Lake Superior, and a sweeping view of the winding St. Louis River.

Elys Peak is a popular rock-climbing destination. The peak was named after Edmund F. Ely, a Presbyterian missionary, postmaster and county commissioner active here in the mid-1800s. According to historian Anne Stutz Bailey, the peak was used by Anishinaabe youth for vision quests.

Chloe crosses Snively Creek (top); and hikers enjoy the exposed and sunny summit of Elys Peak (bottom).

When you've had your fill of the view (or the blueberries), head back the way you came.

The Superior Hiking Trail

It's a gift to hikers. A treasure. It's one of the best long-distance hiking trails in the United States. Its name even says "Superior." The **Superior Hiking Trail** (SHT) brought world-class backcountry hiking to the rugged North Shore, opening up parts of the country few, if any, had ever visited.

The Superior Hiking Trail was built as a rugged, low-impact trail. It winds around trees and maintains natural obstacles, including rocks. Trail designers chose scenery over convenience, running the trail up to overlooks and down to waterfalls rather than straight across the land. Most streams have bridges over them and most wet areas have boardwalks through them. The trail and trailheads are very well marked.

One can walk over 300 miles on a footpath from Jay Cooke State Park to the Canadian border, much of it on the ridgeline overlooking Lake Superior. The Superior Hiking Trail is built and maintained by the Superior Hiking Trail Association, a member-supported nonprofit organization based in Two Harbors. For the latest information about the trail, stop at the Superior Hiking Trail Assn. office on the main street through Two Harbors, or visit **www.superiorhiking.org**.

Explore Spirit Mountain

Take a steep hillside. Throw in some trees. In the winter, sprinkle on some snow. It all adds up to F-U-N at Spirit Mountain.

While Spirit Mountain is a busy hub of outdoor recreation in the winter, visitors are finding more and more activities in the summer. If you love trees and hills, take a ride or two on the Timber Twister, Spirit Mountain's alpine coaster. You ride a sled that's fixed to the rails for a fast and curvy downhill run. German engineering means the ride is smooth, quiet and fun.

There is also a zip line and miniature golf. The Superior Hiking Trail curves around the ski slope, including a spur to the pleasant modern campground. You're sure to stay busy at Spirit Mountain. Learn more at **www.spiritmt.com**.

04 Western Waterfront Trail

A 6.2 mile out-and-back hike along the St. Louis River in Duluth

A fishing dock off the Western Waterfront Trail lets a hiker see the St. Louis River marshes up close.

▶ **What makes it unique.** Right in the City of Duluth, this trail runs along the edge of the scenic and varied St. Louis River estuary. This route starts from the trail's quiet eastern end and follows the entire trail.

▶ **Finding the trailhead.** The most popular access to the trail is at Indian Point, off of Grand Ave. However, it's a better hike starting at this more obscure eastern trailhead. The eastern trailhead at 63rd Ave. West can be reached from the Central Ave. exit of Interstate 35: go south on Central Ave. 0.3 miles to Raleigh St., turn right on Raleigh St. and go 0.5 miles to 63rd Ave. West. Take 63rd Ave. West 0.5 miles south to trailhead on right side. Park on the street.

From the 63rd Ave. West trailhead, this is a six-mile round trip hike along the edge of the historic St. Louis River. Duluth prides itself on being an "urban wilderness," and you'll understand that moniker on this hike.

The trail is wide and graveled, so it's often one of the first dry trails in the spring, and at this time of the year, the river is full of migrating birds. The trail leads through a series of peninsulas and bays. The peninsulas offer a great view of the river, and the bays end with moist bottom lands dominated by huge willow trees.

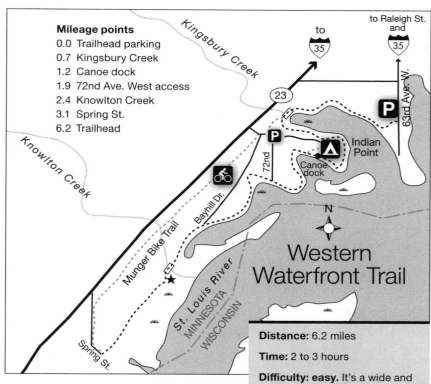

Mileage points
0.0 Trailhead parking
0.7 Kingsbury Creek
1.2 Canoe dock
1.9 72nd Ave. West access
2.4 Knowlton Creek
3.1 Spring St.
6.2 Trailhead

Kingsbury Creek

to (35)

to Raleigh St. and (35)

(23)

63rd Ave. W.

P

P

Indian Point

Canoe dock

72nd

Knowlton Creek

Bayhill Dr.

Munger Bike Trail

St. Louis River

MINNESOTA

WISCONSIN

Spring St.

N

Western Waterfront Trail

Distance: 6.2 miles

Time: 2 to 3 hours

Difficulty: easy. It's a wide and level trail, so the only difficulty will be how long you choose to walk.

More info:
City of Duluth Parks & Rec
www.duluthmn.gov/parks
(218) 730-4300

GPS coordinates:
N46° 43.40'
W092° 10.65'

Trailhead facilities: Vault toilets at Indian Point. None at 63rd Ave. West.

For the first third of a mile, the trail passes private docks and backyards. You're soon into the first bay and to the first huge willows. In the spring, the willows are flush with a golden yellow.

The first creek is Kingsbury Creek. The first peninsula is Indian Point, where there is a campground and the most popular access point. Indian Point became a popular destination for tourists in the early 20th century when the first automobiles brought travelers equipped with tents and cook stoves to Duluth.

After rounding another bay and peninsula, the trail crosses 72nd Ave. West at an historic dock area. The route travels through more developed areas after this and leaves the waterfront behind to follow a dirt road (Bayhill Drive) past a pumping station and across Knowlton Creek. In an open meadow there is a bench and view of Tallis Island. This would be a perfect resting and turn-around spot, making for a 5.7 mile round-trip hike.

To complete the Western Waterfront Trail, continue past the meadow and bench, alongside railroad tracks and past the Tate and Lyle factory. Turn around at Spring St. and return to the trailhead.

❱ **Other options for this hike.** If you'd like to see new scenery on the way back or save time, follow the Western Waterfront Trail all the way to its end on Spring St., turn right and follow Spring St. to Riverside Drive 0.3 miles to the Willard Munger Trail. Turning right and walking on the bike-friendly Munger Trail will take you back to Indian Point and save about a mile on the route.

The Western Waterfront Trail has wide and easy walking right along the bank of the St. Louis River.

Nearby Eats, Treats & Lodging

There are pleasant overnight accommodations right near the Western Waterfront Trail, including the Willard Munger Inn and the historic Indian Point Campground. You'll find pub fare and pleasant surroundings at Spirit Mountain's Riverside Bar & Grill on Grand Avenue.

05 Brewer Park Loop

A 4.2 mile loop hike on the Superior Hiking Trail in Duluth

Enjoy sweeping views of western Duluth and the St. Louis River from this loop trail.

▶ **What makes it unique.** Climb from a rugged river gorge to a loop on top of a dramatic plateau right in the middle of urban Duluth. This is one of the most scenic sections of the Superior Hiking Trail in Duluth.

▶ **Finding the trailhead.** Exit Interstate 35 at Central Ave. (Exit 252) in western Duluth. Take Central Ave. 0.8 miles north to Highland St. Turn left on Highland St. and travel 1.0 miles, driving past Oneota Cemetery on the right. Turn right onto W. Skyline Parkway. Superior Hiking Trail parking lot is immediately on the right.

This hike feels like a highlights video of the Duluth portion of the Superior Hiking Trail, with a rushing creek, historic structures and dramatic views of the city and the St. Louis River.

The trail starts at the far north end of the parking lot. Head straight down to the huge old road bridge that crosses Keene Creek. You'll pass two trails headed off to the right, first the SHT headed to the west and then the Duluth Traverse multipurpose trail. This bridge was once the route for cars on Skyline Parkway and an important connection between Proctor and Duluth.

Like most creekside trails, this first section of the hike is much rougher than the rest of the hike. Steep stream banks are either too rocky or have too much clay

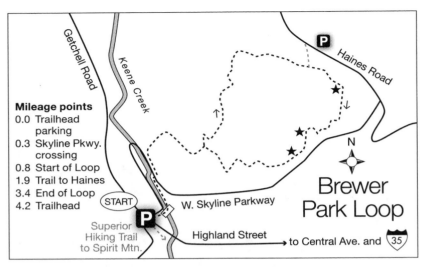

Mileage points
0.0 Trailhead parking
0.3 Skyline Pkwy. crossing
0.8 Start of Loop
1.9 Trail to Haines
3.4 End of Loop
4.2 Trailhead

START

Superior Hiking Trail to Spirit Mtn.

W. Skyline Parkway

Highland Street

to Central Ave. and 35

N

Brewer Park Loop

Distance: 4.2 miles

Time: 1.5 to 2.5 hours

Difficulty: moderate. Rough footing in Keene Creek and gradual but persistent climbs.

More info:
Superior Hiking Trail Assn.
www.superiorhiking.org
(218) 834-2700
Map Series A

GPS coordinates:
N46° 45.01'
W092° 11.24'

Trailhead facilities: None

to hold a good hiking trail. Though difficult, the trail gives you access to a gurgling creek and interesting historic structures, including what looks like an old pump house.

After the trail crosses Skyline Parkway, it crosses a large lowland area using long stretches of boardwalk, then begins to slowly climb and soon reaches the start of the Brewer Park Loop. Stay off the old spur trail on the left at about one half mile that leads back to Skyline Parkway.

The Brewer Park Loop itself is about 2.5 miles long. You can hike it either direction. Turn left at the junction to hike the loop clockwise. This lovely stretch of trail was built in 2016 and meanders past large maple and oak trees, then around exposed bedrock polished smooth by the Ice Age glaciers. It's just over a mile on this new stretch before you reach the far end of the loop.

Soon after the junction, dramatic views begin to open up to the left. For nearly a mile, it's one big view after another. You'll start with open rocky views of the central Duluth hillside and harbor, but soon you're seeing Lake Superior, the Aerial Lift Bridge, Enger Tower, and eventually the entire St. Louis River estuary.

Nearby *Eats,*
Treats &
Lodging

Wussow's Concert Cafe, at 324 N. Central Ave., is right on the way to the trailhead off of Interstate 35. Small but funky, they have coffee, beverages, food and live music to top off your hike.

The last stretch of the loop leads through a magical stretch of park-like woods with tall maple and red oak trees and a ground cover of Pennsylvania sedge. Watch for a tree trunk bent over 90 degrees to make a natural woodland bench, and a large boulder split in half.

Complete the loop and return back off the plateau of Brewer Park to scenic Keene Creek and the trailhead.

❱ **Other options for this hike.** Many hikers start this loop from Haines Road on the east side. This option is shorter and a bit easier. Park at the trailhead parking lot on the east side of Haines Road. The parking lot is 0.4 miles uphill from where Haines Road crosses Skyline Drive. The trail crosses under Haines Road in a tunnel.

The hike follows scenic Keene Creek for about 300 yards (left). Up on the ridges, blue blazes guide the way across exposed bedrock (right).

06 Enger Tower

A 4.6 mile out-and-back hike on the Superior Hiking Trail in Duluth

From Enger Park, hikers discover one of the best views of Duluth and western Lake Superior.

▶ **What makes it unique.** One of three hikes that start right in Canal Park, this takes you to Duluth's historic landmark, Enger Tower, overlooking the harbor and Lake Superior.

▶ **Finding the trailhead.** You can start this hike anywhere in Duluth's Canal Park or Bayfront area. The Minnesota Slip Bridge is the small blue bridge that crosses the slip in which the William Irvin ore boat museum is found, next to the dock for the Vista Fleet. Parking is available in the DECC lot or the lot behind Bellisio's Restaurant and Grandma's Sports Garden in Canal Park.

The trek to the top of Enger Tower has two very different parts. The first half of the hike takes you through highly developed waterfront property. The second half is a traditional forest hiking trail, with a challenging gain of 500 feet in elevation in just one mile. The view from the top of the tower is amazing.

Find your way to the Minnesota Slip Bridge, the start for this hike. Believe it or not, you are now on the Superior Hiking Trail, and you'll find Superior Hiking Trail signage to guide your way. In developed areas like this, small white stickers with the blue and green Superior Hiking Trail logo, often with a blue arrow, mark the trail. You'll find the stickers on metal posts and other surfaces. Follow those signs as the trail winds along a zigzag sidewalk on the edge of the Duluth harbor,

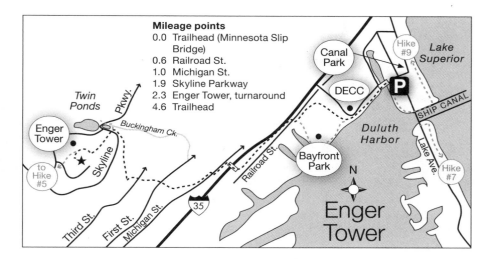

Mileage points
0.0 Trailhead (Minnesota Slip Bridge)
0.6 Railroad St.
1.0 Michigan St.
1.9 Skyline Parkway
2.3 Enger Tower, turnaround
4.6 Trailhead

past Great Lakes Aquarium, to Railroad St. For about 0.4 miles, the SHT shares the route of the bike-friendly Cross City Trail.

After crossing Railroad St., the route runs right under the elevated viaducts of Interstate 35.

The trail climbs a long ramp and then crosses Interstate 35 on a pedestrian bridge. Hang in there—the real hiking is coming soon. Follow the Superior Hiking Trail signs west on Michigan St. and cross at the bus stop bench over to Glen Place. You'll see the dirt trail climbing a knoll off to the left.

Now you're finally hiking on a dirt path in the woods. The trail climbs right into the forest, working its way uphill. This area was heavily quarried for its gabbro rock, and the trail sneaks along the top edge of a few of the quarries. It passes old foundations and climbs old stone steps. The views get better as you climb. The trail crosses abandoned or low-traffic city streets.

In this forested section, keep an eye on the blue Superior Hiking Trail paint blazes to keep you on trail through a young birch forest. After a long traverse you'll reach Buckingham Creek and a tall old retaining wall before emerging on

Distance: 4.6 miles

Time: 2 to 3 hours

Difficulty: moderate. Route finding and road crossing are required, with a significant uphill climb.

More info:
Superior Hiking Trail Assn.
www.superiorhiking.org
(218) 834-2700
Map Series A

GPS coordinates:
N46° 46.88'
W092° 05.73'

Trailhead facilities: Restrooms, restaurants, shops.

Climb up historic stone steps (left) on the way to scenic
Enger Tower (right).

Skyline Parkway right by Twin Ponds.

When the trail reaches Skyline Parkway, look carefully for the blue blazes. There's a junction of a spur trail to the official Superior Hiking Trail trailhead across Twin Ponds. The Duluth Traverse multi-purpose trail also crosses the SHT. Stay on the main trail here and cross Skyline Parkway to stone steps visible across the road. It's just a short jaunt into Enger Park. You can see Enger Tower; work your way there leisurely, enjoying the flower beds and the famous Peace Bell. Enger Tower sits on top of a rock outcrop. Take the stairs to the top, where you can walk around the entire top level for a 360-degree view of Duluth.

See if you can pick out all the landmarks from the top of Enger Tower. Start with a view of the Aerial Lift Bridge and go right, walking around the top of the tower. On a clear day, you can see, from left to right: Aerial Lift Bridge, Apostle Islands, Superior Entry Lighthouse, Minnesota Point, ore docks, Bong Bridge, St. Louis River, Oliver Bridge, Spirit Mountain, Lake Superior College, Enger Golf Course, Duluth Heights water tower, and the Antenna Farm.

▶ **Other options for this hike.** You can keep going on the Superior Hiking Trail through Duluth's Lincoln Park and Piedmont neighborhoods and connect with Brewer Park Loop (Hike #5). Plan ahead and you can catch a city bus back downtown from the Brewer Park trailhead at the intersection of Skyline Parkway and Highland St.

07 Duluth Beach Walk

A 4.6 mile out-and-back hike along the Lake Superior shoreline in Duluth

Duluth's waterfront leads right from the famous Lift Bridge to six miles of public beach.

▶ **What makes it unique.** Hike through one of Minnesota's most unusual habitats, with beach grass and migrating shorebirds and waves lapping at your feet. If you get tired, you can hop on the city bus for the trip back, rather than walk back.

▶ **Finding the trailhead.** Trailhead is the Lake Superior Maritime Visitor Center (aka the Marine Museum) in the heart of Duluth's Canal Park. Reach the trailhead from Interstate 35 Exit 256B. Turn south on Lake Ave. and go straight past clock tower 0.5 miles onto Canal Park Drive. Parking is available near Visitor Center in pay lots.

From a Canal Park hotel room, this hike takes you far, far away—from the busy Canal Park tourist zone to the most seashore-like experience you can have in Minnesota.

Minnesota Point is the seven mile long, 200-yard wide sand spit that begins across Duluth's famed Aerial Lift Bridge from Canal Park. The Point leads all the way to Wisconsin. The seven miles of public beach on the lake side of the Point are a treasure. There is no real trail, just a ribbon of firm sand along the edge of the water.

To reach the beach by foot, cross the Lift Bridge. At the far end of the bridge, take a sharp turn left into the grassy area. Follow the right side of the grassy area to a cement wall. Step down off the cement wall to the beach.

In the far distance, you may be able to pick out the Superior Entry lighthouse, over six miles away. It's all public beach between here and there.

Walking on the beach is perfect for reflection and thinking deep thoughts. The sand dunes here are the only home in Minnesota for a number of plant species, including the locally abundant beach grass.

You'll pass the Franklin Park public access, known locally as the "S-Curve." After Franklin Park, the dunes rise up and you are surrounded by sand and Lake Superior.

Walk as far as you want. Be sure to find a big driftwood log to sit on for a break and watch the waves. In early fall, watch for migrating shorebirds taking a break in their migration between Arctic mud flats and the Gulf of Mexico. If it's hot in July or August, walk in the water or even take a dip in the lake.

You can turn around anytime you want. For this 4.6 mile hike, turn around at Lafayette Square, which is well marked by a large wooden sign. However, if you're having a great time, continue another two miles to the Park Point beach house.

❱ Other options for this hike. The Duluth Transit Authority runs the hourly #15 bus down Park Point from Canal Park. You can take the bus out to its turnaround spot. In summer, the turnaround spot is at the Park Point Beach house. This would give you a 4.2 mile one way hike back to Canal Park.

For a shorter one-way hike (2.4 miles), get off the bus at 31st St., across from the Lafayette Square recreation center, and follow the footpath around the building to the beach access.

Graffiti along the start of the hike (left) contrasts with the sign at the turnaround.

Distance: 4.6 miles

Time: 1.5 to 3 hours

Difficulty: easy.
You'll be walking along the Lake Superior shoreline on soft sand.

More info:
Duluth Parks & Recreation
www.duluthmn.gov/parks
(218) 730-4300

GPS coordinates:
N46° 46.78'
W092° 05.53'

Trailhead facilities: Restrooms, drinking water, museum, restaurants.

Canal Park Hikes

There are three distinctive hikes that leave from Canal Park. Lace up your walking shoes for the climb to Enger Tower (Hike #6). Explore the sandy beach on **Duluth Beach Walk** (Hike #7). Saunter or scamper on the **Downtown Lakewalk** (Hike #9). Duluth is a wild and diverse city, and you are in the heart of it in Canal Park.

(Below) Mike Link and Kate Crowley start their 1,555-mile Full Circle Superior trip in April 2010 along the Duluth beach. See page 35 for their finish.

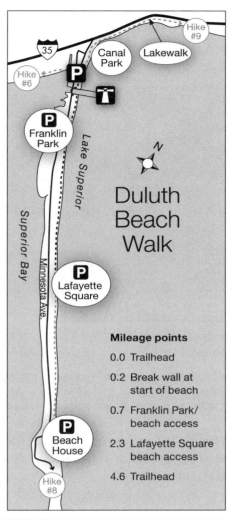

Duluth Beach Walk

Mileage points

0.0 Trailhead

0.2 Break wall at start of beach

0.7 Franklin Park/ beach access

2.3 Lafayette Square beach access

4.6 Trailhead

08 Minnesota Point

A 4.3 mile out-and-back hike through coastal habitats in Duluth

The Minnesota Point Lighthouse, built in 1858, stands in ruins next to the trail.

❱ What makes it unique. If a gorgeous stand of old-growth pine trees isn't enough for you, try sand dune barrens, a lighthouse ruin, and a seven-mile public beach.

❱ Finding the trailhead. From Duluth's Canal Park, cross the Aerial Lift Bridge and travel 4.5 miles to the end of Minnesota Ave. at Sky Harbor Airport. The trailhead is marked by a large sign and a heavy metal gate.

Minnesota Point is a unique geological and ecological environment, and this hike takes you into the best of it.

The mostly flat and straight route takes you through two beautiful pine forests, up and down grassy sand dunes, and past historic maritime structures like the Minnesota's oldest lighthouse and the Superior Entry. If you are very sensitive to poison ivy, you should be careful on this trail as it is surrounded by it.

The first third of a mile of the hike follows a fence between the trail and the runway of Sky Harbor airport. On most pleasant days you'll

Distance: 4.3 miles

Time: 2 to 3 hours

Difficulty: moderate.
Walking in soft sand can be strenuous.

More info:
Duluth Parks & Recreation
www.duluthmn.gov/parks
(218) 730-4300

GPS coordinates:
N46° 43.63'
W092° 02.81'

Trailhead facilities:
Restrooms (at beach house, seasonally).

share this stretch with dogs and their walkers.

At 0.4 miles, the route leads away from the runway and into the first of two stretches of pine forest. The towering white and red pine trees are a great example of coastal conifer forests found only on sandy peninsulas and baymouth bars like this. There are two stretches of pine forest, broken up by pumping stations for Superior's and Cloquet's drinking water. The pine forests are protected as a state Scientific and Natural Area.

The second half of the trail to the Superior Entry is in the dunes and in the coastal barrens. The trail splits and reconnects often as it winds through the dunes and close to the beaches on either side of Minnesota Point. The harbor side, to the right, has numerous quiet and narrow beaches, with warmer water. Walking here can be slow and tiring, as the soft sand gives way underfoot.

This part of Minnesota Point is known as The Barrens, and it's ecologically fascinating, with rare coastal plants like heathers and lichens. Throw in the ruins of the 1858 Minnesota Point Lighthouse and you'll feel like you're in some Gothic novel such as *Wuthering Heights,* calling for Heathcliff. Explore the gloomy ruins of the buoy depot. The giant ore docks that rise from the far side of the harbor add to the moody atmosphere.

Map labels:
to Canal Park
N
Minnesota Point
Superior Bay
Barker's Island
WISCONSIN
MINNESOTA
Lake Superior
Landing strip

Mileage points
0.0 Trailhead
0.9 Water pumping stations
1.6 Old Minnesota Point Lighthouse
2.2 Superior Entry, turnaround
4.3 Trailhead

Pumping stations
Pine forest
SUPERIOR WISCONSIN
1858 Lighthouse ruins
Buoy depot ruins
The Cove
BREAKWATER
Superior Entry

The trail eventually reaches the concrete break walls of the Superior Entry. This is the natural opening to the Duluth-Superior harbor. Unlike the Duluth Ship Canal, here you'll find more ships than tourists. Visible on the other side of the Superior Entry are old buildings owned by the Army Corps of Engineers. Far to the left, at the end of the outer break wall, is the Superior Entry lighthouse, a dramatic orange-roofed white structure.

Tucked between the outer and inner break walls on the Minnesota side is a fun little protected beach known locally as The Cove. Although it's on the Lake Superior side of Minnesota Point, the water is typically warmer here, plus there's always a great collection of driftwood.

▶ **Other options for this hike.** From the Superior Entry you can simply retrace your steps, or you can follow the Lake Superior shoreline along The Cove and the open beach. You might need to bushwhack a bit as the beach pinches out into woods. If the beach walking or the raging waves wear you out, follow one of the frequent trails that cross the dunes back into the pine forest and reconnect with the trail.

Nearby *Eats,* Treats & Lodging

In the summer, the Park Point Beach House offers a lifeguard and swimming beach, refreshments, and the chance to watch or play beach volleyball. During last weekend of June, the Beach House is home to the annual Park Point Art Fair, which features 100+ artisans—their booths nestled next to the dunes. Plan your visit at **parkpointartfair.org**.

Tall white and red pine trees dwarf the trail.

09 Downtown Lakewalk

A 5.8 mile out-and-back hike along the waterfront in Duluth

In 2010, Mike Link completed his 1,555-mile Full Circle Superior hike around Lake Superior on the Lakewalk, where he and Kate Crowley were joined by 200 friends and fans.

▶ **What makes it unique.** Right in the heart of Duluth is the longest stretch of Lake Superior shoreline trail in Minnesota. A hiker can have a great time exploring the nooks and crannies of the shoreline.

▶ **Finding the trailhead.** The Downtown Lakewalk can be accessed from many points in downtown Duluth and its eastern neighborhoods. For the hike described here, you can park and start at the parking lot closest to the Lake Superior Maritime Visitor Center (the "Marine Museum").

This lovely walkway is by far the longest continual lakeshore trail on the North Shore. It's wide and paved and full of people at first, but there are wild places just off the trail to explore.

Find the official start of the Lakewalk in the parking lot closest to the Marine Museum, at the corner opposite the Museum. For the first mile, there are two separate paths: a wooden boardwalk for pedestrians and a paved path for bike riders and in-line skaters. Highlights along this most popular part of the

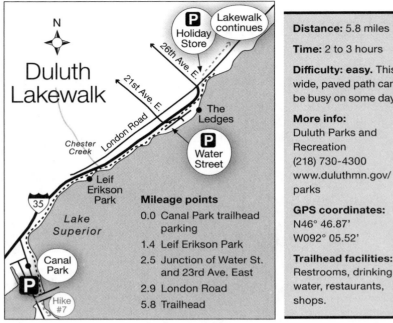

N

Duluth
Lakewalk

P Holiday Store
Lakewalk continues

26th Ave. E.

21st Ave. E.

London Road

The Ledges

P Water Street

Chester Creek

Leif Erikson Park

35

Lake Superior

Canal Park

P

Hike #7

Mileage points

0.0 Canal Park trailhead parking

1.4 Leif Erikson Park

2.5 Junction of Water St. and 23rd Ave. East

2.9 London Road

5.8 Trailhead

Distance: 5.8 miles

Time: 2 to 3 hours

Difficulty: easy. This wide, paved path can be busy on some days.

More info:
Duluth Parks and Recreation
(218) 730-4300
www.duluthmn.gov/parks

GPS coordinates:
N46° 46.87'
W092° 05.52'

Trailhead facilities:
Restrooms, drinking water, restaurants, shops.

Lakewalk include the mysterious Uncle Harvey's Mausoleum, the broad pebble beach at the corner of the lake, and the mosaic mural that features images from Duluth and Lake Superior history. Can you pick out the famous steamer *Mataafa*, which wrecked right off Duluth's piers? The two war memorials provide quiet places for reflection.

Near the end of the boardwalk, two sets of stairs rise up and cross the railroad tracks. The stairs lead to shops and restaurants in the Fitger's complex and the popular Portland Malt Shop.

After the boardwalk ends, walkers and riders share the same path. Hikers will want to take the narrow dirt paths that lead off to the right toward the lake. Nearly every one of these leads to a hidden overlook or private beach.

The Lakewalk cuts through the green amphitheater of Leif Erikson Park. Hikers can veer around to the right along a narrower trail with access to the shoreline, then rejoin the Lakewalk proper.

Past Leif Erikson Park, there is a half-mile stretch of Lakewalk with the busy Interstate 35 and the railroad tracks on your left, and interesting Lake Superior shoreline on your right. Watch for a bedrock point and side trails just past the gurgling outflow of Chester Creek. Wide expanses of bedrock farther on show signs of being carved and smoothed by glacial ice.

At the 2.3-mile mark, the Lakewalk reaches the Beacon Pointe resort area and small parking lot. The Lakewalk continues along the sidewalk of Water St. for a quarter mile.

Past Water St. is the wildest and most beautiful stretch of shoreline of the whole Lakewalk. Watch for informal paths off to the right. They will lead you to The Ledges, a long-time local hangout with rock outcrops and secret cobblestone beaches.

You can return to the paved trail and finish its run along the lakeshore where it runs into the sidewalk of London Road. Shortly before that, the main Lakewalk runs under London Road and up to a trailhead parking area by the Holiday Store on London Road and 26th Ave. East.

▶ **Other options for this hike.** While the Lakewalk officially continues past here, the trail runs through neighborhoods and sidewalks and is much more appropriate for bikes and in-line skates.

Nearby **Eats, Treats & Lodging**

You can step off the Lakewalk for an ice cream cone or a beverage with a view at numerous places, including the Portland Malt Shoppe. At Fitger's, check out Fitger's Brewhouse, Mexico Lindo, or local shops. Don't miss the gelato at Va Bene, a block east of Fitger's on Superior St.

Step off the paved Lakewalk near 23rd Ave. East and discover The Ledges, with hidden beaches and wild North Shore rock gardens.

10 Hartley Nature Center

A 2.2 mile loop hike on the Superior Hiking Trail in Duluth

From the top of Hartley's Rock Knob, the view stretches through wild Duluth to Lake Superior.

▶ **What makes it unique.** Follow this route through Hartley Nature Center's diverse trail system and experience the best of this extensive urban wild area.

▶ **Finding the trailhead.** From Interstate 35, take Exit 258 (21st Ave. East) and travel 0.7 miles up 21st Ave. East to Woodland Ave. Turn right on Woodland Ave. Follow Woodland Ave. 2.4 miles to the Hartley Nature Center entrance on left. Follow entrance road 0.3 miles to main parking lot.

For most of the hikes in this book, you won't need a detailed route description. There are good maps and signs at each intersection. For this one, you'll want to pick up a map and even bring along this book to get you past some tricky turns. The route is a loop combining the main Superior Hiking Trail, a short stretch of the abandoned Hartley Road, and parts of the Duluth Traverse trail.

Start from the Nature Center on the gravel path marked by frequent Superior Hiking Trail signs. The trail parallels Tischer Creek on your left and crosses the Hartley Pond dam. The loop starts after crossing the dam, with a left turn. Follow the Superior Hiking Trail signs and blue paint blazes. A massive windstorm in July 2016 blew down thousands of Hartley's trees. The first half mile of this hike leads through the most devastated area. The trail climbs and rolls along a ridge

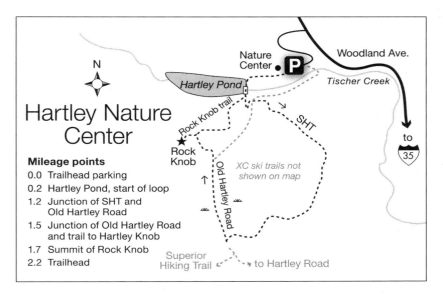

Hartley Nature Center

N

Mileage points
0.0 Trailhead parking
0.2 Hartley Pond, start of loop
1.2 Junction of SHT and
      Old Hartley Road
1.5 Junction of Old Hartley Road
      and trail to Hartley Knob
1.7 Summit of Rock Knob
2.2 Trailhead

Nature Center **P** *Woodland Ave.*

Hartley Pond *Tischer Creek*

Rock Knob trail *SHT*

to 35

Rock Knob

Old Hartley Road

XC ski trails not shown on map

Superior Hiking Trail *to Hartley Road*

top for the next 0.9 miles, crossing the XC ski trails five times. There is an unusual dwarf forest on top of the ridge and partial views down toward Lake Superior.

Turn right at the obvious T-junction at Old Hartley Road (the straight gravel road); the Superior Hiking Trail continues to the left toward UMD's Bagley Nature Area.

This is a large marsh area, an unusual habitat for hilly, rocky Duluth. There's a boardwalk spur trail to the left that leads to a scenic viewpoint of the marsh.

Watch for the Rock Knob trail to the left, as you enter a stand of jack pine trees. The route up is shared with bicycles.

From the saddle, scamper up to the top

Distance: 2.2 miles

Time: 45 to 60 minutes

Difficulty: moderate. Route finding is a bit tricky; there are some steeper climbs.

More info:
Hartley Nature Center
www.hartleynature.org
(218) 724-6735
Map at nature center building

GPS coordinates:
N46° 50.31'
W092° 04.98'

Trailhead facilities: Restrooms, drinking water, and nature center.

of Rock Knob for a 360-degree view of eastern Duluth. Lake Superior is visible in the distance through the West Tischer Creek valley. You are standing in the middle of Hartley Park, and the only signs of civilization are a few mansions on nearby ridges.

Scamper back down to the saddle then follow the "Rock Knob" Duluth Traverse trail along the edge of the ridge. The trail takes you back to Hartley Pond and to the beginning of the loop.

❭ Other options for this hike. You can continue south and west on the Superior Hiking Trail, crossing Arrowhead Road to Bagley Nature Area for a nearly two-mile loop through maple forest before returning. Or follow the Superior Hiking Trail all the way downhill 4.5 miles to the Rose Garden and the Lakewalk.

Nearby Eats, Treats & Lodging

The Hartley Nature Center building is open weekdays and Saturdays. Be sure to check out the exhibits and talk with friendly staff and volunteers. Learn more at **www.hartleynature.org**. Bulldog Pizza & Grill in the Mt. Royal Shopping Center is a great spot to eat for all ages.

The hike starts at the Hartley Nature Center building, where you can enjoy educational displays and pick up a trail map (top); Hartley Pond is a tranquil oasis in the middle of Duluth (bottom).

11 Knife River

A 4.0 mile out-and-back hike along the Knife River in the town of Knife River

Second Falls, 1.0 mile into the hike along the Knife River, roars with spring melt off.

▶ **What makes it unique.** On a stretch of the North Shore not known for hiking and best known for the Expressway zooming past, discover this classic North Shore river hike, complete with waterfalls.

▶ **Finding the trailhead.** From mile marker 18.2 on the Highway 61 Expressway, turn northwest on E. Shilhon Road. The road here is labeled UT 7. After 0.2 miles, the road changes to St. Louis County 255. You'll find the trailhead parking lot on the right, 0.7 miles from the Expressway.

This trail was built in the early 1990s by volunteers of the Superior Hiking Trail Association and was intended to be the western end of the trail. However, in order to connect the Trail from Duluth to Two Harbors, planners found it necessary to route the trail much farther inland. That leaves a Superior Hiking Trail-quality trail in a place very convenient to most North Shore travelers.

The Knife River is one of the largest rivers on the North Shore between Duluth and the Canadian border. Its Ojibwe name is *Makomani-zibi*, related to the sharp rocks in the streambed. Early prospectors found veins of copper in the 1860s, and mining operations were in place by 1899.

Originally, this hiking trail started in the actual village of Knife River, across

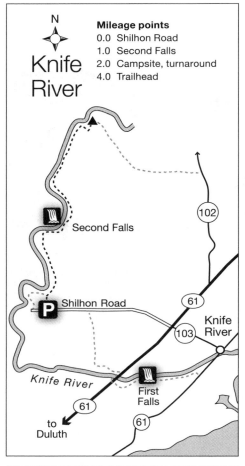

N

Mileage points
0.0 Shilhon Road
1.0 Second Falls
2.0 Campsite, turnaround
4.0 Trailhead

Knife
River

Second Falls

102

Shilhon Road

61

Knife
River

103

Knife River

First
Falls

61

to
Duluth

61

Distance: 4.0 miles round trip

Time: 1.5 to 2 hours

Difficulty: moderate. Hike is mostly level,
although route finding may be difficult.

More info: Knife River Recreation Council
www.kniferiver.org

GPS coordinates:
N46° 57.10'
W091° 48.17'

Trailhead facilities: None

the old scenic highway from
the campground. The trail still
exists but it is rough, unsigned
and unmaintained. It runs past
scenic First Falls and the fish lad-
der. The old trail crosses under
the Expressway bridges and then
leads through the woods up to
Shilhon Road.

From the new trailhead, the
trail follows the rim of the Knife
River gorge and skirts the edge of
a 2011 logging operation. You'll
see young pine and cedar trees
in six-foot high metal cages.
Deer browsing is so severe here
that the only way a white pine
seedling will survive is with
cages like this.

The trail drops down sturdy
wooden steps toward the river.
Watch along this stretch for a
small wooden sign that reads,
"Copper mine 1863," and note
the small hole in the earth behind it. Historians say that only
a few tons of copper were mined
in this region, all in the 1800s.

One mile from the trailhead,
you'll reach Second Falls, a scenic highlight of the day. Eve and
Gary Wallinga, in their book
*Waterfalls of Minnesota's North
Shore*, awarded Second Falls
three out of five stars. For such a
peaceful remote location, there
has been controversy here over

the last few years as the falls have been manipulated to allow easier passage by steelhead and brook trout.

Continue about a mile to a scenic campsite at rapids on the inside of a bend in the river. This is a perfect spot for lunch and a nap. Return the way you came.

▶ **Other options for this hike.** After the rapids campsite, you can keep hiking; the trail continues 0.9 miles to a parking area at County Road 102 (Hawk Hill Road). This last stretch of trail is rather wet, flat and boring in comparison to the previous section.

Nearby **Eats, Treats & Lodging**

Knife River is an old fishing village that has modern amenities. Be sure to check out the sweet treats at Great! Lakes Candy. ■ Food lovers will appreciate the cuisine at The New Scenic Café just a few miles west, or at the Ledgerock Grille at Larsmont a few miles east. ■ In early December, celebrate Julebyen with its ethnic food, artists, decorations, music, and trolls. Hike the Knife River trail and decorate a tree along the way. More at **julebyen.us**.

Explore Old Highway 61

Stoney Point offers a scenic stretch of lakeshore rock hopping and walking along Stoney Point Road.

Which is the real North Shore experience? Is it speeding down the four-lane expressway with virtually no view of the big blue lake? Or is it a quaint two-lane road that winds through little towns? I'd take the two-laner.

Old Highway 61 hugs the Lake Superior coast from Duluth to Two Harbors. Along the way are dozens of little pull-offs and parks that invite you to explore. The grand-daddy of them all is **Kitchi Gammi Park,** also known as "Brighton Beach," on the right as you leave Duluth's city limits. There are smaller pull-offs every mile or so. Each one calls out for exploration.

Recently built is the **McQuade Access.** Developed for boaters, it's actually a fun place for casual visitors as well, with tunnels under the old highway, a pleasant breakwall, and restrooms.

Hikers and nature lovers will find the wildest and most scenic shoreline along this stretch at **Stoney Point,** about a mile east of Homestead Road. Turn off on Stoney Point Road.

12 McCarthy Creek

A 6.2 mile out-and-back hike on the Superior Hiking Trail north of Two Harbors

Chloe enjoys an autumn break in the scenic forest near McCarthy Creek.

▶ **What makes it unique.** This is primarily a walk through the woods and newly-opened logged areas. Tree lovers will notice a gradual progression of forest types and ages.

▶ **Finding the trailhead.** From mile marker 14.8 on the Highway 61 Expressway, turn north on County Road 42 (Homestead Road). Take this 7.2 miles past a T-junction. Turn left on County Road 41 (Culbertson Road and Two Harbors Road). After 2.0 miles, turn left on County Road 266 (Laine Road). Travel north 3.5 miles. At this point, County Road 266 turns sharply left and becomes Rossini Road. Travel another 1.1 miles to the Superior Hiking Trail trailhead parking on left.

This is a lovely, easy walk on the Superior Hiking Trail through the far upper reaches of the Knife River. Since there are few panoramic viewpoints, pay attention to the changing forest around you. If you can consistently identify two specific trees, the sugar maple and the balsam fir, you'll see a lot going on in forest change and succession along this hike.

McCarthy Creek has many small branches, and you will cross at least three branches of the creek on this hike. The destination for this hike is a small waterfall on McCarthy Creek with a footbridge and a nearby campsite.

In spring, you should find a great variety of wildflowers and birds along this

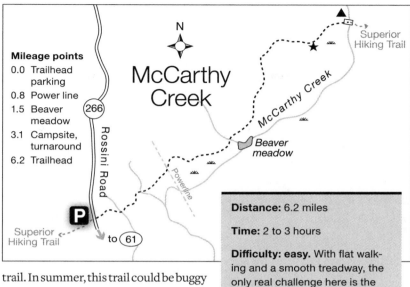

Mileage points

0.0 Trailhead parking
0.8 Power line
1.5 Beaver meadow
3.1 Campsite, turnaround
6.2 Trailhead

Distance: 6.2 miles

Time: 2 to 3 hours

Difficulty: easy. With flat walking and a smooth treadway, the only real challenge here is the length of the hike.

More info:
Superior Hiking Trail Assn.
www.superiorhiking.org
(218) 834-2700
Map Series B

GPS coordinates:
N47° 05.43'
W091° 49.26'

Trailhead facilities: None

trail. In summer, this trail could be buggy and wet. In fall, the colors are excellent and the trail should be dry.

The landscape is glacial end moraine here; tips of the great continental glaciers paused here and dumped their load, leaving small kettles and slightly rolling terrain. The ponds fill up with water and frogs in the spring, and then dry up. The moraine underfoot has also made the trail flatter and smoother than on most Superior Hiking Trail sections.

The trail leaves from Rossini Road (across from the parking lot). After a short stretch of mature forest, the trail enters a large area logged in 2004. The rather poetic name for this sale was the Golden Sunrise. Planted here were 22,000 white spruce seedlings, though you'll notice more balsam fir trees.

Balsam fir trees can grow by the thousands when land is cleared. Later in the hike, you'll see balsam fir trees of all ages, including ancient tall trees and young saplings trying to grow in the shade of maple trees.

The middle part of this hike, after crossing under a power line, is through a beautiful northern hardwood forest. For almost a mile, the trail winds through maple and oak forest. The trail reaches a high point at about 1,660 feet with very

A fascinating face looks out at hikers from a trailside sugar maple.

slight views in the fall season to distant ridges. You can see here why the Superior Hiking Trail Association has added this hike to their list of best fall hikes.

Keep an eye out for the beds of old logging railroads. These were rudimentary narrow-gauge tracks that were only in use for a few years over a century ago, but their impact on the landscape is still visible.

Right before the turnaround point, the trail leaves the maple forest and climbs up a short, steep bank. There's a small view out to the right over a lowland, and the trail crests to the top of what appears to be a glacial esker, a sinuous ridge of gravel left by a river that ran under the glacial ice. Then the trail reaches the McCarthy Creek campsite and waterfall.

Compared to Gooseberry's falls or most other North Shore waterfalls, this waterfall is tiny and grassy, but it's lovely all the same. Take a break on the footbridge or up in the campsite area before beginning your hike back to the trailhead.

Nearby *Eats,* Treats & Lodging

In late July or August, blueberry lovers find their way through these same back roads to Shary's Berries, a pick-your-own organic blueberry field. Call (218) 834-5221.

The Superior Hiking Trail crosses McCarthy Creek right below the waterfall.

13 Lighthouse Point

A 3.2 mile loop hike along the Lake Superior waterfront in Two Harbors

Just a few steps off the wide Sonju Trail, informal trails follow the wild, rocky edge of Lighthouse Point.

▶ **What makes it unique.** Right in the town of Two Harbors, you can combine exploration of the rugged Lake Superior shoreline, a unique breakwater, and artifacts of the 19th century. Along the way, toss in a piece of pie at a local eatery or a microbrew at the local brewery to make your hike even more memorable.

▶ **Finding the trailhead.** Just east of Two Harbors on Highway 61, turn south on Park Road at the Burlington Bay Campground. Just past the campground entrance on the left, park on the paved area above the beach.

If there is room in your heart for a town, this hike may make you fall in love with Two Harbors. Where else can you find secluded gravel beaches, two working lighthouses, a dramatic breakwater, and historic hunks of iron ore in one short hike?

The paved start of the Sonju Trail is marked at the south end of the beach parking area.

Although there are formal trails, half the fun of this hike is getting off the official trail and exploring the lakeshore. Signage is generally nonexistent, but just follow either the wider trail or a route closer to the lakeshore. You'll pass through Lakeview Park, with tall white pines and plenty of benches for resting.

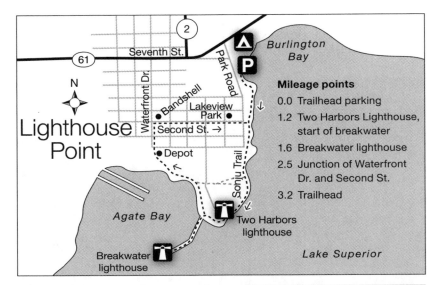

Seventh St.

61

Burlington
Bay

N

Lighthouse
Point

Waterfront Dr.

Park Road

Bandshell

Lakeview
Park

Second St. →

Depot

Sonju Trail

Agate Bay

Breakwater
lighthouse

Two Harbors
lighthouse

Lake Superior

Mileage points

0.0 Trailhead parking

1.2 Two Harbors Lighthouse,
start of breakwater

1.6 Breakwater lighthouse

2.5 Junction of Waterfront
Dr. and Second St.

3.2 Trailhead

Just after passing the Two Harbors water pumping station, you'll turn left off the paved trail onto a narrower gravel trail For 500 glorious yards, between the pumping station and the lighthouse, you can walk on the expansive ledgerock.

Have some fun with this hike. Follow the cobblestone beach to its end and then climb up the rough trail at the far end. Fear not the breakwater with its one cable for a handrail. At the end, hang out downtown with your friends and enjoy a craft beer. It's all good.

The breakwater and the main lighthouse were built in 1892. The breakwater protects Agate Bay, a busy port dominated by the ore docks. It is over 500 yards long and the top surface is flat and plenty wide, even for those afraid of heights or falling into the water. The Two Harbors Breakwater Lighthouse at the end was built in 1897. The views from the breakwater are dramatic, reaching down the shore as far as Knife River and right into the heart of the ore docks.

Distance: 3.2 miles

Time: 1.5 to 2 hours

Difficulty: moderate. While there's a wide, level trail and sidewalks for most of the route, adventurous hikers will also scamper along the beaches and ledgerock.

More info: Lake County Chamber of Commerce (218) 834-6200 www.lakecounty-chamber.com Map at RJ Houle Info Center

GPS coordinates:
N47° 01.48'
W091° 39.69'

Trailhead facilities:
Campground

From the breakwater, you could simply retrace your steps back to the Burlington Bay beach and campground. However, the loop described here is shorter and takes you deep into Two Harbors history.

The route continues along a shoreline interpretive trail, past the boat ramp, and picks up a wide gravel stub of the Sonju Trail leading toward the ore docks. There's a lovely gravel beach hidden here. The hiking path finally ends at Paul Van Hoven Park and Waterfront Drive. Turn right and head for town. The sidewalk takes you right between two historic rail engines and near the Lake County Historical Society in the old depot.

Continue along Waterfront Drive past historic and culinary attractions. Check out the 3M Museum and Thomas Owens Park with its bandshell and historic artifacts. Turn right on Second Avenue and take the sidewalk half a mile back to Park Drive, where you'll reconnect with Lakeview Park, restrooms, and a short spur back to the Sonju Trail and the rocky shore of Burlington Bay.

The Two Harbors breakwater angles out into Lake Superior one-third mile to the lighthouse.

Nearby **Eats, Treats &** **Lodging**
This hike could be a half-day adventure. Identify coastal wildflowers such as cinquefoil and butterwort on the ledgerock. Tour the lighthouse and the other historic exhibits. Visit Castle Danger Brewery in old downtown. Have lunch on a picnic bench along the way. ■ The hike starts and ends at the Burlington Bay Campground, a large, RV-friendly facility that also has tent sites right near the trailhead. This campground is featured in *Camping the North Shore,* by Andrew Slade.

14 Encampment River

A 5.9 mile shuttle hike on the Superior Hiking Trail in Castle Danger

Views go inland forever across the upper Encampment River valley.

▶ **What makes it unique.** There's something special about this hike on the Superior Hiking Trail. It's an introduction to the real, deep North Shore. It's as if you pass through a magic gateway, leaving civilization behind to arrive on the ridges and forests of the wild Shore.

▶ **Finding the trailhead.** From Two Harbors, travel 2.5 miles northeast on Highway 61 to County Road 3. Turn left and travel 2.1 miles to County Road 301 (Fors Road). Travel 0.2 miles on 301 to Superior Hiking Trail trailhead on the left side.

Hiking this trail is like entering the wild North Shore. To get the full effect of this trail, it's best to arrange a vehicle shuttle so you can hike it from west to east. Shuttle options include driving two cars and using the Superior Hiking Shuttle (reservation only).

During spring run-off, it may be impossible to cross the Encampment River, as there is no footbridge. Check the SHT website for current trail conditions: **www.superiorhiking.org/trail-conditions**.

The first 1.1 miles of the trail are rather forgettable, crossing Silver Creek and Wilson's Creek in mixed forest. It's possible to avoid this part if someone can drop you off on County Road 613, 0.8 miles up from Highway 61. "Drop off" is the important concept: there is no parking on the county road.

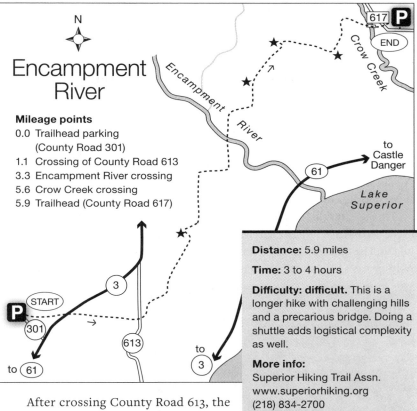

Encampment River

Mileage points

0.0 Trailhead parking
(County Road 301)
1.1 Crossing of County Road 613
3.3 Encampment River crossing
5.6 Crow Creek crossing
5.9 Trailhead (County Road 617)

to
Castle
Danger

*Lake
Superior*

Distance: 5.9 miles

Time: 3 to 4 hours

Difficulty: difficult. This is a longer hike with challenging hills and a precarious bridge. Doing a shuttle adds logistical complexity as well.

More info:
Superior Hiking Trail Assn.
www.superiorhiking.org
(218) 834-2700
Map Series C or McKenzie Map 105: Gooseberry Split Rock

Superior Hiking Shuttle
Call or text (218) 834-5511
www.superiorhikingshuttle.com

GPS coordinates:
N47° 04.58'
W091° 37.51'

Trailhead facilities: None

After crossing County Road 613, the trail begins to climb past large white cedars. You're climbing up a massive outcrop of the Silver Creek Diabase, an erosion-resistant rock. This ridgeline ends on Lake Superior as the famous Silver Cliff, now pierced by a highway tunnel.

There's a beautiful open bluff edge just under a mile in from the county road, with views inland and toward Two Harbors. Here you can sit under a pine tree and take it all in. If you're hiking in and out from Fors Road, this is a good turn-around spot for a 4-mile hike.

The middle stretch of this trail is one of the most unusual trail layouts of the entire Superior Hiking Trail. The trail follows exactly the common border of two property owners. Neither landowner allows trespassing. You'll notice distinct 90-degree turns right and then left as the trail reaches corners of the property. There are beautiful tall white pine trees along the trail, so it's a pleasant walk despite the straightness.

The Encampment River was named for the well-protected bay and landing at the mouth of the river, where early North Shore travelers would camp. In the 1830s, John Jacob Astor's American Fur Company ran commercial fishing from the bay. Proposals for the Encampment River in the early 1900s called for either a new state park or a series of seven hydroelectric dams to bring electricity to Two Harbors. Neither proposal came to be.

Because of frequent flooding, there is no footbridge over the Encampment River, and depending on water levels, you may have to get your feet wet.

On the east side of the Encampment River, the trail climbs sharply to the top of the second major bluff edge, with lots of white pine trees and dramatic views inland. The trail weaves toward and away from the bluff's edge in tall white and red pine trees for about a half mile and is the scenic highlight of the hike. This is a

good destination for a 2.8 mile round-trip hike from the east.

The last mile of the trail weaves down into the Crow Creek Valley. You have now passed through the mythical gateway into the North Shore. The trail descends to Crow Creek itself, in

A bridge crosses dry Crow Creek deep in a rock gorge.

Nearby Eats, Treats & Lodging

This route could be described as the "North Shore Pie Connector," with Betty's Pies and Rustic Inn at the trailheads. Start or end your day with one of their fine creations. ∎ Take a moment midway through the car shuttle to park the car and walk up the Gitchi Gami Trail to Silver Cliff. There's a large parking area on the east side of the tunnel and a very scenic short stroll up the old highway bed to the cliff's edge. Old-timers remember when goats used to graze on the steep cliff above the old road.

a deep and steep basalt gorge. You might see why Crow Creek has been known as "Prohibition Creek," since the creek bed is so gravelly the water sometimes runs underneath and the river appears "dry." From Crow Creek, the trail climbs up to cross County Road 617 and reaches the Superior Hiking Trail's Castle Danger trailhead.

❯ **Other options for this hike.** See Hike #15 for the route east on the Superior Hiking Trail from here up the Crow Creek valley. The Superior Hiking Trail also runs west from here, up scenic Silver Creek, and eventually goes 5.4 miles to the Reeves Road trailhead on County Road 2, north of Two Harbors.

Hard rocks and high points: "diabase" is dark colored

After a billion years of erosion from wind and water and glaciers, the highest points in the North Shore landscape are often the hardest and most resistant to erosion. In the western North Shore, those hard, high points are often composed of a rock called diabase.

Diabase rock has the same "ingredients" as basalt, and is common on the North Shore, especially in the stretch from Silver Creek to Silver Bay. The massive cliffs of Silver Cliff are made of diabase, as is the overlook at Bean and Bear lakes (Hike #21). Unlike the dark fine-grained basalt from lava flows common on North Shore ledge rock shores, diabase is medium-grained and formed underground.

Natural **NORTH SHORE** *Wonders*

Enjoy the views from atop diabase high points at Encampment River (Hike #14), Wolf Rock (Hike #15), Fault Line Ridge (Hike #20), Mount Josephine (Hike #48) and the scenic overlook off the Middle Falls trail at Grand Portage State Park (Hike #50).

Diabase cliffs rise above Bear Lake along Hike #21.

15 Crow Creek Valley

A 2.5 mile out-and-back hike on the Superior Hiking Trail near Castle Danger

Pants tucked in socks during spring tick season, Andrew looks out toward Lake Superior from atop Wolf Rock.

▶ **What makes it unique.** This short bit of the Superior Hiking Trail packs a big variety of terrain and views into a short stretch of trail.

▶ **Finding the trailhead.** From Highway 61 at mile marker 36.7, turn north on County Road 106 (West Castle Danger Road). The turn is just west of the Rustic Inn. Go straight on the road, which becomes Silver Creek Township Road 617. Drive a total of 2.3 miles from Highway 61 to Superior Hiking Trail parking lot on right.

This hike takes you to the top of dramatic Wolf Rock and then another mile inland along the valley of Crow Creek to a scenic overlook at the end of a quiet spur trail.

The Superior Hiking Trail goes both directions out of the parking lot. You'll go east, following the sign for Nester Grade and Gooseberry Falls. Steep Wolf Rock nearly overhangs the trail, challenging you to climb it. The trail winds among outcrops and pine trees as it climbs.

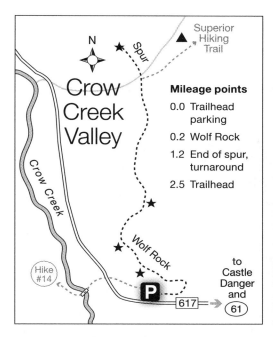

to
Castle
Danger
and

Distance: 2.5 miles

Time: 1.5 to 2.5 hours

Difficulty: moderate.
Some steep and rocky
climbs at the start, otherwise the trail is fairly level
and walking is easy.

More info:
Superior Hiking Trail Assn.
www.superiorhiking.org
(218) 834-2700
Map Series C or
McKenzie Map 105:
Gooseberry Split Rock

GPS coordinates:
N47° 06.77'
W091° 33.43'

Trailhead facilities: None

The view of Lake Superior keeps getting better as you climb. Geologists can tell you that this cliff is composed of diabase, the same erosion-resistant rock that makes up the cliff of the Silver Cliff Tunnel. Wolf Rock was named by trail builders, who heard wolf howls while camped nearby.

After three dramatic viewpoints, the trail turns inland up the Crow Creek valley. The trail rolls up and over bare rock exposures with views of the lake and river valley through old-growth white pine trees off to the left. At one point, there's even a surprising view of the lake off to the right.

The spur junction is obvious...in fact, you'll continue straight ahead while the main trail takes a hard turn to the right. Watch for a pleasant little creek right after the junction; in the spring, the creek provides a great up-close view of yellow marsh-marigolds. It's just a few hundred yards on the spur to the final overlook. Here the view is nearly all Crow Creek valley; Lake Superior is just a blue line in a distant notch.

After taking it all in, return the way you came.

▶ **Other options for this hike.** This is the start of a 9.1 mile through-hike on the Superior Hiking Trail to Gooseberry Falls State Park. This section can be a long trudge through dense forest until the trail opens up on the Gooseberry River, 4.7

miles in. This hike works really well using the Superior Hiking Shuttle (218-834-5511, **www.superiorhikingshuttle.com**). Park at the Crow Creek trailhead and hike to the park, then pick up the shuttle mid-afternoon to get back to your car.

Going west on the Superior Hiking Trail from the trailhead gets you onto Hike #14. It's just a half mile before you descend into the Crow Creek valley and its unique canyon with steep walls. This is a fun place to explore up and down the creek, especially in low water.

Descending from Wolf Rock (above). Fern fiddleheads (top right) and marsh-marigolds (bottom right) grace the trail in spring.

Nearby Eats, Treats & Lodging

The hike completes the other end of the "North Shore Pie Connector route," which starts at Encampment River (see sidebar on page 52). The Rustic Inn is a great stop for food and pie, and even has a gift shop.

16 Five Falls Loop

A 3.0 mile loop hike in Gooseberry Falls State Park, near Castle Danger

Middle Falls of the Gooseberry River is just one of the five fascinating waterfalls in Gooseberry Falls State Park.

▶ **What makes it unique.** Gooseberry Falls State Park is known for its five waterfalls. This trail gets you off the beaten path quickly and lets you explore all five.

▶ **Finding the trailhead.** Gooseberry Falls State Park is located 13 miles northeast of Two Harbors along Highway 61, near mile marker 39. This trail starts at the State Park Visitor Center, a short stroll from the parking lot.

If you like waterfalls, this is the hike for you. Get up close and personal with all five of the park's waterfalls as you follow the shore of the Gooseberry River up one side and down the other.

The first three falls of the Gooseberry River are Lower Falls, Middle Falls (the star attraction of the main viewing area) and Upper Falls. Fifth Falls is the top of this loop. But where is the fourth falls? Maybe you can figure it out as you hike.

The trickiest part of this hike is finding your way out of the Visitor Center area and onto the hiking trail. Follow the crowds toward the main falls viewing area along the paved path, but take the left fork for Upper Falls. After that, follow signs for Fifth Falls Snowshoe Trail.

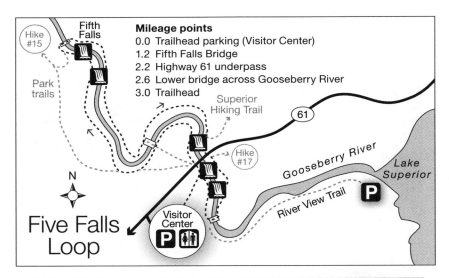

Mileage points
0.0 Trailhead parking (Visitor Center)
1.2 Fifth Falls Bridge
2.2 Highway 61 underpass
2.6 Lower bridge across Gooseberry River
3.0 Trailhead

Five Falls Loop

This trail is best taken clockwise. The trail along the west bank is rougher than on the east side, and you can start with the hard part while you're fresh. Plus you get the grand finale of the lower two falls at the end. The paved trail ends after 0.2 miles at Upper Falls, and the crowds will thin out right away.

The hike up the west side crosses a flood plain then climbs up around a steep bank and briefly follows a XC ski trail. Fun ledges along the river's edge call out for exploration. There's an old three-sided log shelter that could be your destination on a rainy day.

Right before crossing the Fifth Falls Bridge, this route joins the Superior Hiking Trail then stays with it for almost a mile down the east side of the river. The trail along the east side is wider and better maintained. Unlike the west side, the little side trails here lead to dangerous overhangs, not fun play areas. Benches let you sit and absorb the scenic views.

The views get spectacular as the trail crosses under the Highway 61 bridge

Distance: 3.0 miles

Time: 1 to 2 hours

Difficulty: moderate. This is a good family hike for active kids. There are a few hills and slippery spots on the trail.

More info:
Gooseberry Falls State Park
(218) 834-3855
www.dnr.state.mn.us/state_parks/gooseberry_falls
Map available at Visitor Center

GPS coordinates:
N47° 08.38'
W091° 28.19'

Trailhead facilities: Restrooms, campground (nearby), drinking water, store, Visitor Center.

and follows a well-constructed set of steps and cliff-edge bridges high above Middle and Lower Falls. Complete the loop on the Falls View Trail, crossing two stems of the Gooseberry River below dramatic Lower Falls on footbridges. As you pass the main crowded viewing area at Middle Falls, take pride in having experienced the park more fully and deeply than 95% of its visitors.

▶ **Other options for this hike.** You can access this loop from the campground or the Lakeview Picnic Shelter. Follow signs for the River View Trail, which leads from the mouth of the Gooseberry River upstream. This will add about one mile to the overall hike.

For a longer hike of about 4.5 miles, combine this hike with the Gitchi Gummi Trail (Hike #17).

Nearby **Eats, Treats & Lodging**

Visit the exhibits at the Visitor Center and take in a film or a ranger program. Gooseberry Falls State Park has a modern campground with hot showers and very pleasant sites—though no RV hook-ups—and is featured in *Camping the North Shore*, by Andrew Slade.

Explore Gooseberry Falls State Park

Gooseberry Falls is the most popular state park on the North Shore and one of the most visited parks in Minnesota. Most visitors start their park experience with the short walk down to **Middle Falls,** and then end it with a trip to the extensive nature store in the Visitor Center—but there's much more park to explore. Hike #16 takes you through the heart of the park, including to four other waterfalls; Hike #17 to the eastern shoreline, away from park roads.

In addition to these hikes, there's another 15 miles of trails in the park. You can explore the park's backcountry on the Superior Hiking Trail.

Be sure to visit the lakeshore picnic area, known as **Picnic Flow** (pictured above). It's a massive expanse of bare basalt rock, pocked with splash pools and dotted with coastal wildflowers. You'll need a vehicle permit to reach Picnic Flow and the picnic area. Follow the park road to the large parking lot at its end and walk up to find the picnic area.

17 Gitchi Gummi Trail

A 2.0 mile loop hike in Gooseberry Falls State Park near Castle Danger

At the far end of the Gitchi Gummi Trail, viewing platforms are like your own private Lake Superior deck.

▶ **What makes it unique.** While Gooseberry Falls State Park is the most-visited North Shore state park, this hike gets you away from the crowds and into a scenic and historic corner of the park.

▶ **Finding the trailhead.** Gooseberry Falls State Park is located 13 miles northeast of Two Harbors along Highway 61, near mile marker 39. This trail starts at the State Park Visitor Center, a short stroll from the parking lot.

It's North Shore history all wrapped up in a loop trail. This easy hike brings you to numerous viewpoints of Lake Superior and the Gooseberry River, while passing interesting artifacts of the Civilian Conservation Corps (CCC) era. From 1934 to 1941, CCC crews built many of the structures and trails of the park we know today.

This is Gooseberry Falls State Park's Hiking Club Trail, so bring your passport and watch for the password.

Gitchi Gami or Gitchi Gummi? Two trails inside Gooseberry Falls State Park have nearly the same name. This hiking trail is called "Gitchi Gummi." The new paved state bike trail is named "Gitchi Gami." The pronunciation is also different. Longfellow's poem "Song of Hiawatha" mentions the shore of

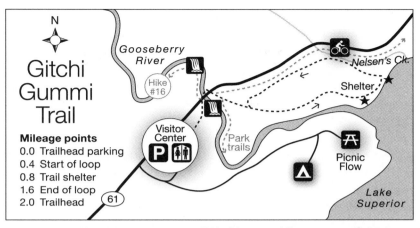

Gitchi Gummi Trail

N

Gooseberry River
Hike #16

Nelsen's Ck.

Shelter

Visitor Center
Park trails

Picnic Flow

Mileage points
0.0 Trailhead parking
0.4 Start of loop
0.8 Trail shelter
1.6 End of loop
2.0 Trailhead

61

Lake Superior

Distance: 2.0 miles

Time: 45 minutes to 1.5 hours

Difficulty: easy. This is a good family hike. The trail is mostly level and well-built.

More info:
Gooseberry Falls State Park
(218) 595-7100
www.dnr.state.mn.us/state_parks/gooseberry_falls
Map available at Visitor Center

GPS coordinates:
N47° 08.38'
W091° 28.19'

Trailhead facilities: Restrooms, campground (nearby), drinking water, store, Visitor Center.

"Gitchi Gummi," pronounced *GOO-me.* The last syllables of the bike trail name are pronounced *GAH-me.*

This trail starts on the left of the two trails headed toward the river. Most of the foot traffic from the Gooseberry Falls Visitor Center is headed for the waterfalls. While the falls are a must-see, they aren't on this loop.

Your first sign of the CCC is a statue of a strapping young CCC worker, commemorating their work here and across the state of Minnesota in the 1930s.

You'll follow Hiking Club Trail signs along the way around the loop. Keep a sharp eye out along the first quarter-mile, since there are lots of intersections. The route takes you across the Gooseberry River on a platform attached to the bottom of the Highway 61 bridge. Eventually the signs lead you onto the Gitchi Gummi Snowshoe Trail.

The actual loop starts at about 0.4 miles into the hike, after climbing up and through stone walls built by the CCC. You can go either way around the loop. The loop takes you past a dramatic stone shelter and a less dramatic but still historic outhouse, apparently "the only CCC outhouse still in existence." The trail follows the edge of 100-foot cliffs dropping off directly into Lake Superior, with great viewing platforms. History buffs will appreciate the stumps of massive white pine trees that once stood here.

Enjoy different views of Nelsen's Creek on the backside of the loop, including the small waterfall just downstream from where the trail meets the creek. The backside of the loop gets a bit confusing as the trail winds past the eight-foot-high deer exclosure fences.

▶ **Other options for this hike.** This trail is linked with many other loops and shortcuts in the 20-mile system of trails at Gooseberry Falls State Park. Rather than return the way you crossed the river, head down the Falls Trail to the lower bridge crossing of the river. This gives you a great view of more waterfalls as the Gooseberry River cascades down to Lake Superior. Or, connect this hike with Five Falls Loop (Hike #16) for a 4.5 mile adventure.

Explore Twin Points

It's North Shore history…in reverse. Halfway between Gooseberry Falls and Split Rock Lighthouse State Parks you will find a wonderful little piece of the wild North Shore. But it wasn't always so wild. Today, Twin Points offers a Lake Superior boat launch, Iona's Beach Scientific and Natural Area, and easy access to the Gitchi Gami bike trail.

Turn off Highway 61 at mile marker 43.0. **Iona's Beach** is reached by a short walk through a pine plantation. The beach is composed exclusively of rhyolite cobblestones drawn off a nearby cliff. Since it's exposed to Lake Superior's northeaster storms, the beach is steeply angled down to the water.

Natural **NORTH SHORE** *Wonders*

Take the time to walk around the shoreline. What looks like a well-preserved natural area was for decades the site of the Lind family's Twin Points Resort. The land came to the state of Minnesota through a complicated land swap that also involved the North Shore's Sugarloaf Cove and Taconite Harbor.

Iona's Beach is made up entirely of red shingle rocks.

18 Split Rock River Loop

A 5.0 mile loop hike on the Superior Hiking Trail near Beaver Bay

Andrew heads downstream along the upper Split Rock River, where it runs smooth and easy before plunging through the red rock gorge.

▶ **What makes it unique.** Get to know the red rhyolite rock in a gorgeous gorge on this easy-to-reach Superior Hiking Trail loop.

▶ **Finding the trailhead.** 17 miles northeast of Two Harbors on Highway 61, at mile marker 43.2, enter the large parking lot on the west side of the Split Rock River.

Because of its easy access off Highway 61 and because it's a loop, this is one of the most popular hikes on the Superior Hiking Trail. On fall weekends, the large parking lot will fill up and cars will overflow onto Highway 61.

The trail is also popular because it penetrates a spectacular red rock gorge and passes lovely waterfalls, and the hike wraps up with one of the better views of Lake Superior on this part of the North Shore. There are so many waterfalls they are mostly unnamed and unnumbered.

The two sides of the loop are very different, and you should plan accordingly. The west side (closer to Duluth) runs deep in the valley of the Split Rock River, on the north- and east- facing slopes that get little sunshine. The trail here is often slippery and steep.

The east side of the loop (closer to Grand Marais) is a bit longer but much

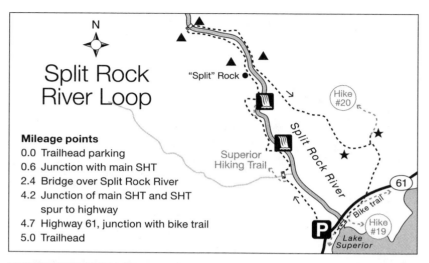

Split Rock River Loop

"Split" Rock

Hike #20

Superior Hiking Trail

Split Rock River

Hike #19

61

Bike trail

P

Lake Superior

Mileage points
0.0 Trailhead parking
0.6 Junction with main SHT
2.4 Bridge over Split Rock River
4.2 Junction of main SHT and SHT
spur to highway
4.7 Highway 61, junction with bike trail
5.0 Trailhead

Distance: 5.0 miles

Time: 2 to 4 hours

Difficulty: difficult. This is a challenging trail. The west side's steep clay banks can get slippery. And without a bridge to cross the Split Rock River at the top of the loop, hikers might get their feet wet. Be careful during spring run-off or after heavy rainstorms.

More info:
Superior Hiking Trail Assn.
www.superiorhiking.org
(218) 834-2700
Map Series C or map available at state park office

GPS coordinates:
N47° 10.93'
W091° 24.55'

Trailhead facilities: restrooms, campground (nearby), drinking water, store, Visitor Center.

easier to hike. The terrain is higher and drier, and the views open up to the far shores of Lake Superior.

The trail starts as a spur of the Superior Hiking Trail. There are many dying birch trees, leaving good views of the river valley below. After a half mile, the spur trail meets the main Superior Hiking Trail coming in from Gooseberry Falls State Park. You'll follow the main trail, now marked with blue paint blazes.

Along the west side of the river, you'll find bridges, boardwalks and timbers trying to keep the trail in place on the clay banks. The first waterfall is on a side creek, the west branch of the Split Rock. The trail reaches the main branch of the river 0.8 miles in, where you'll find big cedar trees and a ledge of rock with a distant view of a waterfall upstream.

The second time the trail reaches the river is at the lower end of a spectacular gorge made entirely of a massive flow of rhyolite, visible across the river in a cliff. Rhyolite has the same mineral

Twin rhyolite pillars along the trail may be the origin of the name "Split Rock."

ingredients as granite, but the crystals are so small that the rock looks red. The rock fractures on clean, sharp lines. Those sharp rocks underfoot and in the cliffs and pillars may be the origin of the name "Split Rock."

The trail dips down to visit two more waterfalls in the red gorge. You can surround yourself in red rhyolite inside two remarkable pillars, which frame a view of more waterfalls below. The pillars may also be the "split rock."

Above the rhyolite gorge, the trail levels out and passes two campsites. Cross the river at the former bridge site, though be careful during spring run-off or after heavy rainstorms.

The second half of the loop follows the east side of the river above the same gorgeous rhyolite gorge. The trail is flatter, drier and much easier hiking. Take the short spur down to the SE Split Rock River campsite, and notice the two pillars high up on the other of the river.

The trail climbs just a bit to reach big and bigger views of the river valley and Lake Superior. Along an open ridgeline, you can see across Lake Superior to the Apostle Islands. There's a lean-to shelter close to the area of the big view.

To see the famed Split Rock Lighthouse: at the junction of the main Superior Hiking Trail with the spur back down to Highway 61, turn left onto the main trail about 50 yards to an open ridgeline and you'll have a view east along the shoreline to the Lighthouse.

The trail makes a big, straight descent to Highway 61. Cross the highway and turn right on the Gitchi Gami bike trail. A pedestrian tunnel under Highway 61 returns you to the trailhead parking lot.

▶ **Other options for this hike.** Try overnight backpacking and use one of the four campsites above the gorge.

19 Corundum Point Trail

A 2.7 mile in-and-out hike in Split Rock Lighthouse State Park near Beaver Bay

The view from on top of Corundum Point is one of the best on the Lake Superior shoreline.

▶ **What makes it unique.** Split Rock Lighthouse State Park has the longest stretch of accessible Lake Superior shoreline of any Minnesota park. From beaches to rocky overlooks, this route takes full advantage of the dramatic coastal environment.

▶ **Finding the trailhead.** Go to Split Rock Lighthouse State Park and historic site, 21 miles northeast of Two Harbors on Highway 61. After obtaining your vehicle permit at the park office, turn right on the park road with signs for the Campground and Trail Center. Follow this road 0.4 miles and turn left into the Trail Center.

▶ **Minnesota State Park vehicle permit required.**

When most North Shore visitors think of Split Rock Lighthouse, the first (and only) thing that comes to mind is the historic lighthouse itself, which is a true Minnesota icon. But that one busy tourist site is surrounded on all sides by some of the most rugged Lake Superior coastline of the entire Minnesota shore. This hike takes you right along that shoreline to a particularly dramatic high point.

Start at the Trail Center, where you'll find restrooms and shelter. This is the State Park Hiking Club trail, and you'll pick up the blue Hiking Club signs right

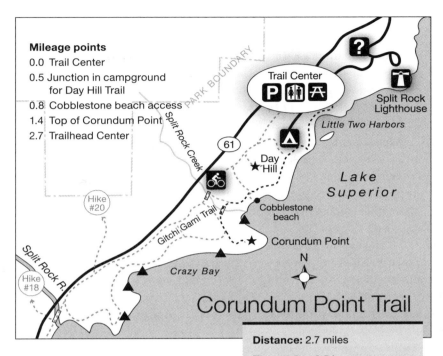

Trail Center

Split Rock Lighthouse

Little Two Harbors

61

Day Hill

Lake Superior

Hike #20

Cobblestone beach

Corundum Point

Gitchi Gami Trail

Crazy Bay

N

Split Rock Creek

Split Rock R.

Hike #18

PARK BOUNDARY

Corundum Point Trail

from the shelter. You'll start on the gravel Little Two Harbors Trail. This was named after a settlement that thrived in this protected bay. The trail continues around the cobblestone beach of the bay, soon offering the first view of the lighthouse.

The route leads through Split Rock's cart-in campground, and you'll see some very appealing campsites. If you're not camping here now, you'll wish you were.

In the middle of the campground, the trail splits. Take the left turn, toward campsites 11-20. You'll follow the Hiking Club signs backward onto the Day Hill Trail. Basically, you'll take every left turn (except to campsites) you can take on the way to Corundum Point.

At the far end of the campground, the

Distance: 2.7 miles

Time: 1.5 to 2.5 hours

Difficulty: moderate. Route finding is a bit tricky and there are steep stairs, but otherwise the trail is level and easy.

More info:
Split Rock Lighthouse
State Park
(218) 595-7625
www.dnr.state.mn.us/state_
parks/split_rock_lighthouse
Map available at park office or
McKenzie Map 105: Gooseberry
Split Rock

GPS coordinates:
N47° 11.93'
W91° 22.54'

Trailhead facilities: Restrooms, campground, drinking water, covered and indoor picnic areas.

trail becomes narrow and more like a hiking trail. A sturdy staircase with multiple platforms is built into the rocky flank of Day Hill itself; 132 steps lead down toward the water. After turning left at a ski trail, you'll quickly find a short trail that leads to two secluded cobblestone beaches and a great view of Corundum Point.

The trail veers away from the shoreline for a bit and crosses pretty, gurgling Split Rock Creek. Still going backward with the signage, you'll stay on the Hiking Club trail past numerous trail junctions.

About a quarter mile past Split Rock Creek, watch for the junction of the trail to the Corundum Mine Site.

The Corundum Point trail leads first to an interpretive sign and mining artifacts in about 100 yards; a less maintained and more challenging trail takes you another 150 yards to the top of Corundum Point, with open rock exposures and the best views of the day.

Like many other state park trails, this route uses grassy trails that are maintained for XC skiing in the winter. The best time to hike this trail is in the fall, after the grass has been mowed and the ground is dry.

After taking in all the views from Corundum Point, head back downhill and retrace your steps to Little Two Harbors Bay and the trailhead.

Hikers work their way down and around Day Hill.

❱ **Other options for this hike.** This is not the full Hiking Club Trail for the park. To earn the mileage, you have to hike the 5.8 mile loop that runs west on the Gitchi Gami bike trail and then sweeps back around the shoreline. There are backpack campsites along here, and if no one is camping there they make great spots for a lunch break or swim. Site #3 even has its own private beach on Crazy Bay.

A detailed geologic explanation of the Corundum Point Trail hike can be found in *Gooseberry Falls to Grand Portage*, from Ron Morton and Steve Morse.

Explore Split Rock Lighthouse

If there were a prize for "Best Lakeshore in a North Shore State Park," Split Rock Lighthouse would be the runaway winner. At 2,103 acres, it's not the biggest state park on the shore, but it has more Lake Superior shoreline access than any other park. There are five miles of shoreline, at least eleven access points including campsites and beaches, and two of the most dramatic overlooks around. And that's all outside of the busy Split Rock Lighthouse Historic Site, administered by the Minnesota Historical Society.

Besides Hikes #18, 19 and 20, which crisscross the state park, there are other destinations for the adventure-minded park visitor. Climb **Day Hill** from the Trail Center area or from the campground. Don your scuba or snorkel gear and visit the wreck of the **Madeira** off of Gold Rock Point...with permission from the State Park office beforehand. Explore the mouth of the Split Rock River from the new wayside rest, which comes complete with a tunnel under Highway 61 for access to both hiking and biking trails.

The picnic area at Little Two Harbors is a great spot for a long lunch break.

20 Beaver Bay to Split Rock

A 10.6 mile shuttle hike on the Superior Hiking Trail near Beaver Bay

The trail climbs to many ridges like this one, with gradual climbs up one side and steep drops off the back.

▶ **What makes it unique.** This is one of the longest and most challenging sections of the Superior Hiking Trail. The terrain is worth the hard work, with sweeping views, ever-changing terrain, and fascinating pockets of flora and fauna.

▶ **Finding the trailhead.** The western trailhead is the wayside rest right off Highway 61 at the Split Rock River, mile marker 43.2. If you're using the Superior Hiking Shuttle, this is where you should park and meet the van. This route starts at the eastern trailhead, just north of Beaver Bay. From mile marker 51.1 on Highway 61, take County Road 4 (Lax Lake Road) 0.8 miles north to parking lot on right side.

Ready for a challenge? This is the second-longest section of the Superior Hiking Trail, and compared to the longer section, this one has more hills, so it's one of the most difficult as well.

The scenic highlights of the trail are the fault line ridges in the eastern half and the sweeping views down to Split Rock Lighthouse near the western end. The remoteness of the trail means you'll have plenty to see along the way, including wolf scat and some very busy beavers. Hiking from east to west gives you an advantage, since the eastern trailhead is about 300 feet higher than the western trailhead.

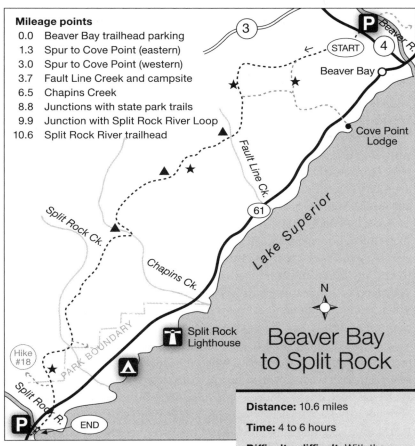

3

START 4

Beaver Bay

Cove Point Lodge

Fault Line Ck.

61

Lake Superior

Split Rock Ck.

Chapins Ck.

N

Split Rock Lighthouse

Hike #18

PARK BOUNDARY

Split Rock R.

END

Beaver Bay to Split Rock

Distance: 10.6 miles

Time: 4 to 6 hours

Difficulty: difficult. With the long distance to hike, the steep hills, and the rough footing, this is a hike for grown-ups.

More info:
Superior Hiking Trail Assn.
www.superiorhiking.org
(218) 834-2700
Map Series C

GPS coordinates:
N47° 15.96'
W091° 18.57'

Trailhead facilities: None

From the Beaver Bay trailhead, the hike starts with a gradual climb. You'll notice bedrock underfoot; it appears that you're climbing up a huge slab of rock with a few trees and moss growing on its surface. The climb ends at the edge of the slab, and the trail descends steeply down the back edge of the slab to a creek. That pattern—gradual ascent on bedrock and steep descent to a wet lowland—happens five times on this hike. You can count the climbs and cliffs to mark your progress for the day. You'll climb almost 1,000 feet over six hills.

Unless you're a lake view connoisseur, you can skip the spur trail marked by the mossy overlook sign. This spur trail has been incorporated into a loop trail from Cove Point Lodge on Highway 61. The overlook is 0.2 miles in and is not all that great; you'll have better views all along the route.

The first summit brings you to an unnamed ridge with views back toward Lake Superior and the steam plume from Northshore Mining. The views, mostly of a rugged valley with mining railroad tracks, continue as you hike. You may hear trains.

Fault Line Ridge (named by geologist and hiker John Green) is the next big cliff you reach. The ridge parallels Fault Line Creek and leads away from the tracks. You'll pass the next junction with the Cove Point loop trail while still traversing Fault Line Ridge. When you hit Fault Line Creek and its beaver pond campsite, you know it will be time to climb again.

Nearby Eats, Treats & Lodging

Beaver Bay has many interesting tourist detours. The Beaver Bay mini-mall has a bit of everything, from ice cream to Christmas decorations. The rock shop is a museum, with fascinating mineral samples and all the authentic Lake Superior agates you could want.

Past Fault Line Creek, be ready to climb up and down three more times and cross two more beaver-rich creeks. A gorgeous stretch of white pine trees comes at about the half-way point of the hike. Christmas Tree Ridge is more subtle than Fault Line Ridge. Chapins Ridge is a real ridgeline, with the terrain dropping off on both sides; the bedrock here has a luxurious carpet of caribou lichen. Geologist Ron Morton calls this high ground Agate Flow Ridge, because of the many agates still in place in the basalt flows underfoot.

The route follows the Merrill Grade for about a half mile. Merrill Grade is the bed of a white pine logging railroad used between 1902-1906, and though the tracks are long gone the trail is still wide and level. Watch carefully for intersections as the Superior Hiking Trail meets Split Rock Lighthouse State Park trails and crosses Split Rock Creek (the much-smaller sister of the Split Rock River farther west).

A brutal climb up (especially challenging after nine miles of hiking) takes you up to the last ridge top and overlooks of the hike. You hike for a quarter-mile on an open, rocky knoll with wide views of Lake Superior, including iconic Split Rock Lighthouse in the distance. Right after this scenic stretch, the route meets the very popular Split Rock River Loop (Hike #18). You'll follow the Superior Hiking Trail spur trail down to Highway 61.

At Highway 61, take a breath and cross the highway. Enjoy your last stretch of hiking along the paved Gitchi-Gami Trail, take a swim at the mouth of the Split Rock River, and return to your car through the pedestrian tunnel under the highway.

Wow, what a day!

▶ **Other options for this hike.** You can hike right into the heart of this route and enjoy some of its remote ruggedness on the six-mile Cove Point Loop. Not only can you skip needing to arrange the shuttle, you can also enjoy Scandinavian hospitality at Cove Point Lodge.

There are good in-and-out hikes from both ends of the trail. From the Split Rock River trailhead, hike 1.0 mile in to the open ridge with views of the lake and lighthouse, for a two-mile round-trip hike. From the Beaver Bay trailhead, there are great views along Fault Line Ridge, perfect destinations for a five- or six-mile round trip.

Andrew explores the crest of Christmas Tree Ridge (top); boulders mark the trail on its steep descents (left); wolf scat along the remote trail (right);

21 Twin Lakes Trail

A 7.5 mile loop hike on the Superior Hiking Trail in Silver Bay

Bean Lake hides in a bowl behind Bear Lake in this unusual view of both "twin" lakes.

▶ **What makes it unique.** Leaving right from the heart of the North Shore's second largest town, this Silver Bay trail is one of the more rugged and scenic. The views of Bean and Bear lakes are incomparable.

▶ **Finding the trailhead.** From Highway 61 at mile marker 54.2, enter Silver Bay on County Road 5 (Outer Drive). Continue 0.4 miles to Bay Area Historical Society information center on right. Trail leaves from far side of parking lot.

The "twin" lakes Bean and Bear are the highlight of this hike and are one of the North Shore's most popular hiking destinations. The lakes are the high point of the 3.1 mile main loop. This main loop has two possible accesses: this Twin Lakes trailhead and the main Superior Hiking Trail trailhead off of Penn Boulevard.

Using the Twin Lakes trailhead instead of the main Superior Hiking Trail trailhead provides more views, a bit more solitude, and more time in gorgeous maple forests. It also makes for a hike that's about two miles longer.

The first quarter mile of the trail requires keeping your eyes wide open. The route follows an ATV trail past backyards and across Banks Boulevard. Watch carefully to find the Twin Lakes Trail where it leaves the ATV trail to your right.

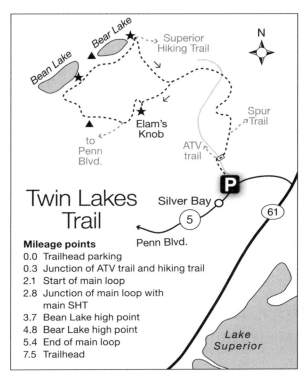

Twin Lakes Trail

Mileage points
0.0 Trailhead parking
0.3 Junction of ATV trail and hiking trail
2.1 Start of main loop
2.8 Junction of main loop with main SHT
3.7 Bean Lake high point
4.8 Bear Lake high point
5.4 End of main loop
7.5 Trailhead

Nearby *Eats, Treats & Lodging*

Silver Bay has a number of restaurants. The Northwoods Family Grille has traditional home cooking. Jimmy's Pizza is in an old Dairy Queen building. ∎ While in Silver Bay, take time to visit the Marina. ∎ Silver Bay has two motels, the Mariner Motel and the AmericInn. Visit **www.visitsilverbaymn.com** for more info.

Distance: 7.5 miles

Time: 2.5 to 4 hours

Difficulty: difficult. Long climbs and rocky terrain makes this a challenging hike.

More info:
Superior Hiking Trail Assn.
www.superiorhiking.org
(218) 834-2700
Map Series C
Map also available at Tettegouche State Park office.

GPS coordinates:
N47° 17.70'
W091° 16.12'

Trailhead facilities: Restrooms (seasonal).

Once you've made that right-hand turn, the rest of the route is well-marked and easy to follow. It's a steady uphill through mixed forest, crossing three wide, multiple-use trails. Silver Bay is visible off to the left; the town gets more and more distant as you climb, eventually disappearing into the rugged folds of the North Shore.

The forest turns to mostly sugar maple after a mile. At 2.1 miles, you reach the start of the main loop. Go left on the West Spur Trail and take the loop clockwise.

Highlights of the main loop are Elam's Knob (a 100-yard climb to a great Lake

Superior overlook, named after local trail builder Bruce Elam), Bean Lake (a 32-acre lake, stocked with rainbow trout, in a deep rocky bowl) and smaller Bear Lake (also deep and in a cliff-lined pocket). Take your time at each one of these for pictures, naps and snacks. For Bear Lake, you'll want to hike all the way to the northeast end of the lake and out on a short spur for the best view of both lakes (see photo page 74).

After Bear Lake, it's a 2.7 mile hike mostly downhill back to Silver Bay. Enjoy the rolling maple forests and the gradual return to civilization.

▶ **Other options for this hike.** You can also reach Bean and Bear Lakes from the Superior Hiking Trail trailhead on Penn Boulevard, north and west of Silver Bay.

You can hike the Superior Hiking Trail east of Bear Lake all the way to Tettegouche State Park; this is a long, challenging and scenic hike that requires a car shuttle—and a lot of energy.

Explore Tettegouche State Park

From the cliffs of **Bean and Bear Lakes** to the open rock expanse of **Shovel Point,** from the scenic quiet of **MicMac Lake's cabins** to the dramatic promontory

of **Palisade Head,** Tettegouche State Park is a vast park with a lot going on for nearly everyone. At 9,346 acres, it is the fourth largest state park in Minnesota.

Hikers will find 23 miles of trails, including Hikes #21, 22, and 23. The Superior Hiking Trail runs for nearly 11 rugged miles

High Falls is the tallest waterfall within Minnesota's borders.

through the park, past landmarks such as **Mount Trudee** and **High Falls** (pictured above), the tallest waterfall completely within Minnesota borders. **Bird watchers** seek rare warblers and nesting falcons. **Campers** can choose from drive-in campsites with hot showers to cart-in sites along the dramatic shoreline…or they can leave their tent at home and stay in one of the park's five rental cabins.

"Tettegouche" is supposedly named after the Algonquin word for "retreat." Escape from the busy world; retreat to Tettegouche.

22 Shovel Point

A 1.3 mile loop hike in Tettegouche State Park, near Silver Bay

State Park
Hiking
Club
TRAIL

Shovel Point rises in the distance as viewed from the Lake Superior Beach spur trail.

▶ **What makes it unique.** This is the most dramatic shoreline trail on the entire North Shore.

▶ **Finding the trailhead.** At mile marker 58.5, a few miles east of Silver Bay, enter Tettegouche State Park. Follow the signs to the right for the Wayside Rest parking area for cars. The trail starts behind the Visitor Center.

This is the shortest, and maybe the sweetest, of all the North Shore Hiking Club trails. The shoreline views are dramatic as the trail climbs up and around the rhyolite cliffs of Shovel Point. There are four developed overlooks, but the whole trail is a scenic wonder. It's a lollipop loop, with a stem of about one-third mile to reach Shovel Point and a loop of one-half mile on top of the Point.

Gather your hiking group behind the Visitor Center, then head straight to the lake on the wide trail. The first views at cliff's edge are stunning. Follow the wide paved trail to the left and head down multiple steps into the shoreline forest. The forest floor has classic North Shore plants, such as thimbleberry and tall lungwort.

The short spur after about 200 yards takes you to Lake Superior Beach, a

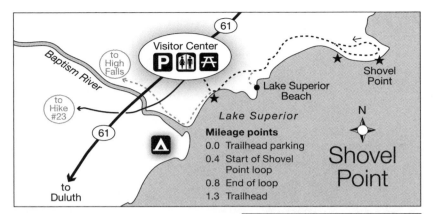

Mileage points
0.0 Trailhead parking
0.4 Start of Shovel Point loop
0.8 End of loop
1.3 Trailhead

Shovel Point

cobblestone beach. A lone pillar stands off the beach, the remains of an arch that fell in 2010.

Take your time on the way in to Shovel Point to visit each of the short boardwalks that lead to overlooks. You'll see Palisade Head looming large a few miles to the west. Palisade Head and Shovel Point were both formed from one huge flow of rhyolite.

The trail makes a counterclockwise loop around the top of Shovel Point, starting along the edge of the cliff and headed downhill to the tip of the Point. This is fragile terrain; the trees and shrubs have grown atop bare rock. That fragility is why the park has built so many boardwalks here, to protect both you and the ecosystem.

Distance: 1.3 miles

Time: 45 minutes to 1 hour

Difficulty: easy. This is a short hike with plenty of handrails and viewing platforms. The hills all have steps built into the trail.

More info:
Tettegouche State Park
www.dnr.state.mn.us/state_
parks/tettegouche
(218) 226-6365
Map at park office

GPS coordinates:
N47° 20.35'
W091° 11.80'

Trailhead facilities: Restrooms, Visitor Center, campground (nearby).

On the way down the edge of Shovel Point, you'll notice the wooden platforms and anchors installed for rock climbers who flock to Shovel Point for climbs named "Dance of the Sugar-Plump Faeries" or "A Study in Scarlet."

A favorite part of the hike is the open exposed rock at the tip of the point and the well-engineered observation deck, where you'll find the Hiking Club password. Not to give the password away, but geologists think this password is misleading.

From the big observation deck, continue along the backside of the loop, through the storm-bent woods back to the top of Shovel Point, then back to the trailhead.

▶ **Other options for this hike.** After returning from Shovel Point, keep walking along the cliff edge to the mouth of the Baptism River. From there you can get away from the crowds and head up the east bank of the Baptism River to High Falls.

Nearby **Eats, Treats & Lodging** — Tettegouche State Park has great camping with two very distinct campgrounds: the 13-site cart-in Lake Superior Campground and the 28-site drive-in Baptism River Campground. Visit **reservemn.usedirect.com/ MinnesotaWeb/** for reservations. For complete camping information, see *Camping the North Shore* by Andrew Slade.

Explore Palisade Head

In all of the North Shore's scenic shoreline, this is the single most dramatic meeting of land and water. Sheer cliffs of red rock rise 200 feet out of Lake Superior. The view from Palisade Head stretches clear across Lake Superior. Distant ore boats look tiny as they pass on their way to Duluth.

Natural **NORTH SHORE** *Wonders*

The geologic event that formed Palisade Head also formed distant Shovel Point. In fact, it was a huge explosion of frothy magma that may have totaled 20 cubic miles.

Known in the 1800s as the Great Palisade, it's been a landmark for centuries. Rock climbers test themselves on the sheer cliffs. Hikers find an unusual North Shore forest of stunted pine trees.

Finding Palisade Head. Turn off Highway 61 at mile marker 57.1, between Silver Bay and the main entrance to Tettegouche State Park. Palisade Head is actually part of the state park. The access road is narrow and winding; you'll need to leave your trailer down by the highway. From the summit parking area, you can wander down to the cliff edge or up the sloping hillside past the radio tower. In late July and August, bring a container and look for blueberries. Just watch your step.

23 Tettegouche Lakes Loop

A 10.1 mile loop hike in Tettegouche State Park, near Silver Bay

Tettegouche Lake sits in a forested bowl, with Lake Superior off in the distance.

▶ **What makes it unique.** One of the longest loop hikes on the North Shore, this hike is a physical challenge and a scenic reward.

▶ **Finding the trailhead.** Enter Tettegouche State Park at mile marker 58.5 east of Silver Bay. With a park vehicle permit, follow the main park road 1.5 miles to the trail parking lot.

▶ **State Park vehicle permit required.**

Do you like a long hike through the woods? Or do you prefer scenic viewpoints? This hike offers both.

The hike runs past all five of Tettegouche State Park's inland lakes: Micmac, Tettegouche, Lax, Nicado and Nipisiquit. The route includes wide grassy state park XC ski trails, narrower state park hiking trails and two miles of the Superior Hiking Trail. There are ten spur trails, and you can pick and choose from them. The best and most scenic are Palisade Valley, Mt. Baldy and Tettegouche Lake.

After a short hike on the main XC ski trail leaving the trail center parking area, you reach an intersection, labeled Junction B. Turn left onto the Superior Hiking Trail here, which you'll follow for two miles as it climbs upward. Sometimes it's a gentle climb. Sometimes it's a brutal climb—like the Drainpipe, a steep cleft in a cliff.

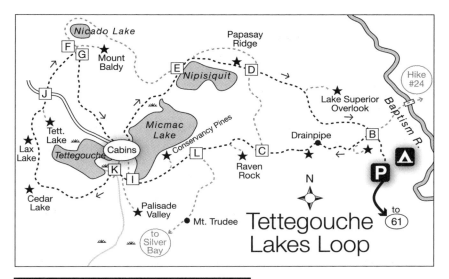

Tettegouche Lakes Loop

Distance: 10.1 miles, plus 2.3 miles of optional spur trails

Time: 4 to 7 hours

Difficulty: difficult. This is a long, challenging hike that requires route finding, at least 900 feet of elevation gain, and Class 3 climbing up the Drainpipe.

More info:
Tettegouche State Park
www.dnr.state.mn.us/state_parks/tettegouche
(218) 353-8800. Map at park office.

GPS coordinates:
N47° 20.68'
W091° 12.86'

Trailhead facilities: Vault toilet, campground.

Mileage points

0.0   Trailhead parking

0.3   Junction B, start of loop

2.0   Junction L, SHT and park trails

2.7   Junction K

4.9   Junction J, road crossing

5.4   Junction F, spur to Mt. Baldy

6.4   Tettegouche Camp cabins

7.7   Junction E, Sawtooth Mtn. Tr.

9.8   Junction B, end of loop

10.1 Trailhead

Along the Superior Hiking Trail portion of the hike, there are two spur trails that lead off to the left. The first isn't labeled. Don't bother with this one: the regular trail will take you to a similar viewpoint soon. The spur to Raven Rock comes after a mile of steady climbing past the Drainpipe. It's 0.3 miles in and out on the spur to an open, rocky overlook of surrounding terrain.

After Raven Rock, the Superior Hiking Trail is more level and runs through older sugar maple forest. Watch for the important Junction L. Here the Superior

Hiking Trail turns left and this route continues forward, on a state park hiking trail. The short spur to Conservancy Pines comes quickly; it leads to tall pine trees and a partial view of Micmac Lake far below. Continue along the main trail and watch for views of the high ridgeline of Mt. Trudee through the trees to the left.

The trail junctions come frequently during this stretch. They are generally well marked and have maps with "You Are Here." Head left at Junction I, then after 90 yards you'll reach the spur to Palisade Valley Overlook. This 0.2-mile spur is long but rewarding, leading to a 180-degree view of the Palisade Valley.

One of the most pleasant surprises of this hike is the unnamed waterfall just ahead. The trail climbs up the side of the waterfall right before Junction K. After passing the waterfall, the trail climbs up into an extensive oak forest, an unusual North Shore habitat.

There are three overlook spurs along this stretch of trail, all short. The Cedar Lake Overlook is the least interesting, since you'll see almost the same view and more at the Lax Lake Overlook a quarter mile ahead. The Tettegouche Lake Overlook is one of the day's highlights, with views of both inland Tettegouche Lake and big Lake Superior as well. Use caution just past the Lax Lake Overlook spur; there's a trail intersection that may be unmarked: the left-hand trail is a dead-end down to Lax Lake.

The hike crosses a wide gravel road at Junction J. This is the main non-motorized access to Tettegouche Camp. You'll continue straight ahead, along a narrow and winding trail through oak and maple trees, and past big boulders.

At Junction G, go left just 40 yards to Junction F. This is the start of the Mount Baldy spur. It's a quarter mile in to this overlook, definitely a must-do as this is the highest and best view of the day. Be sure to check out the short spur trail off the main spur trail, as it gives you a interesting view down to little Nicado Lake far below.

You're headed for Nipisiquit Lake eventually. Here you've got an important choice. Long and easy? Or short and tough? The Sawtooth Mountain Trail continues around Nicado Lake and reaches Nipisiquit in about 1.5 miles. This trail is not always maintained, and may still have a sign that reads "Minimum Maintenance Trail: Expect Poor Conditions." This trail leads across a beaver dam and to another overlook. That's the short and tough way. If you plan to go that way, check before heading out with the Tettegouche park office for current conditions.

The long and easy way to Nipisiquit runs 2.3 miles, starting down the XC ski trail to Tettegouche Camp, on the shore of Micmac Lake. Here you'll find rental cabins and a trail shelter open to the public. Past the Camp you're on wider XC ski trail, with a boardwalk and a big view of tall cliffs.

Nearby *Eats,* Treats & Lodging

The rustic, walk-in Tettegouche Camp cabins are a great base camp for the big wilderness of Tettegouche State Park. Reserve them up to a year in advance at **reservemn. usedirect.com/ MinnesotaWeb**.

After you reach Nipisiquit Lake and continue on the XC ski trail, take the hiking trail that veers off right to Papasay Ridge. Watch for the short spur left to an overlook, where you can see off to the east up the North Shore ridgeline toward Wolf Ridge and Section 13 (Hike #25). Just past Papasay Ridge is large confusing Junction D, as wide XC ski trails and a snowmobile trail converge near the east end of Nipisiquit. You'll go left-ish, following signs for hiking and XC skiing.

This is the homestretch now, down a wide XC ski trail. If you have energy for one last spur trail, head 0.3 miles in to the Lake Superior Overlook. It's the longest spur of the day, and it's great for taking in the whole terrain you've been hiking.

▶ **Other options for this hike.** If you're staying in a cabin at Tettegouche Camp, you could do a modified version of this hike starting from camp.

The elusive Black-throated Blue Warbler

Warblers are the colorful little songbirds that arrive each May on the North Shore, either on their way to points north or coming here to stay and nest in the diverse forests of the North Shore terrain.

The Black-throated Blue Warbler is one of the rarest of these birds. In Minnesota, it is only found along the North Shore. This warbler nests in the shaded understory of the North Shore's sugar maple and oak forest. While rare, its population is considered stable.

The best place to look for the Black-throated Blue Warbler is in Tettegouche State Park. Try the Mount Baldy Trail (on Hike #23), or the short trail from Tettegouche Camp to Mosquito Creek. Look for thin maple trees and scattered oak trees, with brush for nesting. Another place to look is the Oberg Mountain trail (Hike #34).

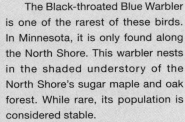

Natural **NORTH SHORE** *Wonders*

24 Wolf Ridge Fantasia

A 7.1 mile shuttle hike on the Superior Hiking Trail near Little Marais

The trail passes Wolf Lake; if you look carefully, you can pick out wind turbines on the far ridge.

▶ **What makes it unique.** This is one of the more challenging mid-length sections of the Superior Hiking Trail. Spur trails to unusual destinations give the adventurous hiker greater rewards.

▶ **Finding the trailhead.** To meet the shuttle, park at the western trailhead, 0.8 miles from Highway 61 on Highway 1. This hike starts at the eastern trailhead. From Highway 61 at mile marker 65.3, take County Road 3 (Little Marais Road) 2.3 miles to parking area on right.

Plan your day for a fun and challenging hike. You'll climb almost 1,000 vertical feet to dramatic overlooks and deep maple forests. Make sure you have time and energy to take in both of the signed spur trails, to Picnic Rock and Fantasia. The spurs add an extra mile and are both extraordinary.

Interestingly, some of the only signs of civilization you'll see on this hike are wind turbines. There's one in the scenic homestead valley of Crystal Bay township and one at Wolf Ridge Environmental Learning Center.

The first half of the hike alternates between rocky climbs to scenic views and long level stretches through thick, old sugar maple forest. The second half has more birch trees and is more rolling.

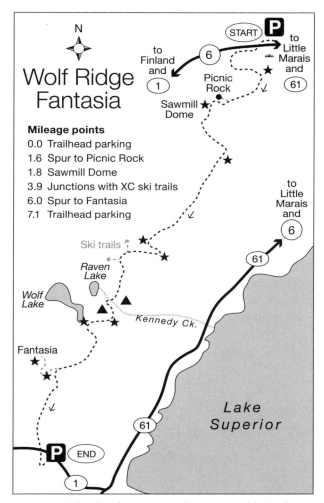

Wolf Ridge Fantasia

Mileage points
0.0 Trailhead parking
1.6 Spur to Picnic Rock
1.8 Sawmill Dome
3.9 Junctions with XC ski trails
6.0 Spur to Fantasia
7.1 Trailhead parking

From the parking lot on County Road 6, it's a one-third mile road walk to the Superior Hiking Trail on the left. The long climb to Sawmill Dome runs through a fascinating landscape riddled by giant boulders and blanketed by maples. The views begin right away, off to the right and then off to the left. There are steep drop-offs here, so keep an eye on children and dogs.

The spur to Picnic Rock is just 200 yards long, to a jumble of massive rock slabs that form a tunnel, a picnic table, and other interesting formations. Back on the trail, you'll soon reach Sawmill Dome and its wide views. The anorthosite rock here is popular with rock climbers.

The middle part of the trail takes you through property owned and managed by Wolf Ridge ELC. There are great views up and down the North Shore, as far as Taconite Harbor and Sugarloaf Cove to the east and to Palisade Head on the west. The ELC has been restoring white pine trees where the birch trees are dying out; the trail briefly follows ELC XC ski trails in that decaying birch forest. Don't miss the view across Wolf Lake inland to the ELC campus.

The 0.4 mile spur trail to the Fantasia overlooks is a special treat near the end of your hike. It's a gradual climb yielding more views, including the fascinating Fantasia area, where you take in a beaver pond below and a jumble of smooth rock, cliffs and trees off to the right.

The long descent to the Highway 1 trailhead is your victory march as you complete this physically challenging hike.

▶ **Other options for this hike.** If you can't set up a car shuttle, you can still do a great in-and-out hike from either trailhead.

From County Road 6, it's a diverse and challenging 3.2 mile round trip hike to Sawmill Dome, with dramatic views along the entire route. Take the extra time to explore Picnic Rock on the way up, and enjoy the view from Sawmill Dome.

From Highway 1, make the 2.9 mile round trip to Fantasia.

Distance: 7.1 miles, plus spur trails

Time: 3 to 5 hours

Difficulty: difficult. Although the length of the hike is only mid-distance, the climbs and descents make it challenging.

More info:
Superior Hiking Trail Assn.
www.superiorhiking.org
(218) 834-2700
Map Series C or
McKenzie Map 104: Beaver Bay, Tettegouche

GPS coordinates:
N47° 24.76'
W091° 09.06'

Trailhead facilities: None

Car shuttles make for rewarding hikes

Of the 50 hikes in this book, at least five of them are meant to be car shuttle hikes. These hikes are one-way treks with good road access at both ends. Sure, you could hike them in-and-out, but it feels great to hike from Point A to Point B.

Most people arrange shuttles by having two or more cars. The two drivers meet at the end point of the hike, where everyone fits into one car and drives to the start of the hike. At the end of the hike, everyone gets back in their own cars; one person has to drive the shuttle car driver back to the start of the hike.

A number of local businesses offer excellent hiker shuttle services:

• **The Superior Hiking Shuttle**—Fridays through Sundays, May through October, plus year-round specialized service. www.superiorhikingshuttle.com or (218) 834-5511.

• **Harriet Quarles Transportation**—spring through fall, (218) 370-9164, harrietq@boreal.org or www.harrietquarles.com.

If you're staying at a North Shore lodge, ask at the front desk to see if they'll do a vehicle shuttle for you as part of their guest services.

25 Section 13

A 2.6 mile out-and-back hike on the Superior Hiking Trail near Little Marais

From the rounded domes atop Section 13 cliffs, the view stretches inland for miles.

❱ **What makes it unique.** Get up close and personal with the dramatic cliffs and rugged terrain of classic anorthosite cliffs.

❱ **Finding the trailhead.** From Highway 61 at mile marker 65.3, take County Road 6 (Little Marais Road) 2.3 miles to parking area on right.

Once a secret spot cherished by rock climbers, the Section 13 cliffs are now a popular day hike destination. Some hikers will continue past the cliffs on the Superior Hiking Trail, bound for the Finland Rec Center, but most will enjoy the cliffs and return.

From the parking lot, the trail disappears into a thick forest of fir and birch. The trail runs flat for a while, following boardwalks, before crossing Sawmill Creek and beginning a gradual climb.

This is where the hike gets really interesting. As you climb, the forest gradually changes from birch and fir trees to maple and oak trees. There's an ephemeral pool on the right: it's wet with frogs in spring, dry and grassy in the

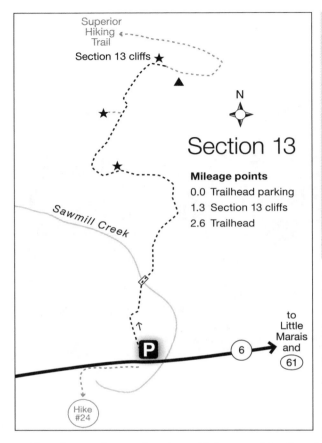

Superior
Hiking
Trail

Section 13 cliffs ★

N

Section 13

Mileage points

0.0 Trailhead parking
1.3 Section 13 cliffs
2.6 Trailhead

Sawmill Creek

to
Little
Marais
and
61

P

6

Hike
#24

Nearby Eats, Treats & Lodging

The Finland historic site is a collection of historic buildings from the area; the Finland Coop has everything you need for post-hike goodies. Both are a few miles farther up County Road 6.

fall. The climb gets pretty steep at times, but each steep climb is rewarded by a terrific view out across the broad valley of Sawmill Creek. Be sure to take the 40-yard spur to the left just before reaching the crest. There's a 135-degree view that pulls in everything from Lake Superior far to the left and the town of Finland far to the right.

The big climb ends at the top of the Section 13 cliffs. This is a fantastic place to hang out and enjoy the views. The open anorthosite rock is bare and smooth and invites scampering. Just don't scamper right off the edge; it's at least a 70-foot drop to the rough talus slope below. You can see why, long before the Superior Hiking Trail, rock climbers would bushwhack in to reach this site. The climbs have creative names, like "Macho Pitchu" and "Rubble Trouble."

Why is it called "Section 13?" That's how early rock climbers could locate this place on a topographic map. Each township is divided up into 36 one-mile square sections, which are numbered 1 through 36. These cliffs are located in section 13 of this particular township.

Distance: 2.6 miles

Time: 1 to 2 hours

Difficulty: moderate.
If climbing uphill 500 feet in one mile doesn't tire you out, climbing back down will.

More info:
Superior Hiking Trail Assn.
www.superiorhiking.org
(218) 834-2700
Map Series D or McKenzie Map 104: Beaver Bay, Tettegouche

GPS coordinates:
N47° 24.70'
W091° 09.25'

Trailhead facilities: None

(Right) The trail to the Section 13 cliffs passes through birch and maple and is especially lovely in the fall.

From the top of the Section 13 cliffs, the view encompasses the dramatic ridgeline that includes Wolf Ridge ELC, the wide Sawmill Creek Valley, nearby beaver ponds, and a rocky hill to the right covered in pine trees—your next destination.

On a clear day, look for a gap in the surrounding ridges where you can look through to the distant North Shore, all the way to the Grand Marais area. Using a compass, look out at 61 degrees.

This lovely and open ledgerock could be the turnaround point for your hike, but consider walking just a little further along the trail. You'll pass a SHT campsite on the right, where you'll find a shady sitting area and a wilderness latrine. Another 100 yards or so, after a small dip, there's a small knoll you can climb on top of, and on top you'll find a huge viewpoint, with 270 degrees of distant landscape views.

Take another few minutes on top of the Section 13 cliffs to ponder the landscape before descending through the oak and maple forest and returning to the trailhead.

26 Eighteen Lake

A 2.7 mile loop hike in the Superior National Forest near Isabella

The trail runs completely around Eighteen Lake, seen here from its northern end.

▶ **What makes it unique.** This remote trail is part of the "Lake District," three shorter hikes around lakes in the Superior National Forest. This one has gorgeous white and red pine trees and scenic benches for rests.

▶ **Finding the trailhead.** From the town of Finland, take Highway 1 north 16.1 miles to Isabella. Turn right on Forest Road 172 (Wanless Road). After 0.8 miles, turn left (north) on Forest Road 369 (Sawbill Landing Road). At 1.6 miles, watch for "Recreation Site Eighteen Lake" sign. Turn left on Forest Road 369E. Drive 0.6 miles to the rustic campground and trailhead.

This pleasant and varied loop circles Eighteen Lake, a walleye lake near Isabella. The trailhead is right next to a small rustic Superior National Forest campground, in a beautiful grove of white and red pine trees. The trail is mostly level, though there are three or four hills to climb. Four benches are conveniently located around the loop.

Go either direction from the trailhead along the shore of the lake. In the park-like pine forest that dominates the eastern lakeshore, the forest floor is covered with pine needles. In either direction, you'll reach the first of four

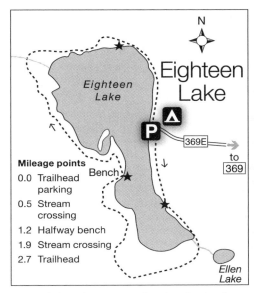

Distance: 2.7 miles

Time: 60 to 90 minutes

Difficulty: easy. The footing is occasionally rough with boulders. It's a great adventure for families staying in the campground.

More info:
Tofte Ranger District
(218) 663-8060, tofte@fs.fed.us

GPS coordinates:
N47° 38.60'
W091° 20.66'

Trailhead facilities: Vault toilet, campground, canoe launch (Eighteen Lake).

Mileage points
0.0 Trailhead parking
0.5 Stream crossing
1.2 Halfway bench
1.9 Stream crossing
2.7 Trailhead

sturdy benches soon. The pine forests here are the scenic highlight of the trip. The northern half of the loop is hillier and rougher than the southern half.

At both the south and north ends of the lake, the trail leaves the lakeshore and runs around wetter areas (a cedar forest at the south end, an alder grove at the north end).

The forest on the west side is much younger and more mixed, with birch and balsam trees instead of pine trees. The forest away from the lake was recently thinned, leaving many standing white pine trees for ecological succession. The footing is a bit rockier on the west side.

The halfway point around the loop is marked by a bench out on a piney point across from the trailhead. Watch for a huge white pine just north of the halfway bench, towering over a quiet bay of the lake that is ringed by cedars.

▶ **Other options for this hike.** Make a day of it by visiting the next "Lake District" trail, at Divide Lake (Hike #27).

Nearby Eats, Treats & Lodging

Trout anglers will find many brook trout lakes nearby. There is a remote and quiet Superior National Forest rustic campground at Eighteen Lake with just three sites in a shady forest of white and red pine trees. You'll likely have Eighteen Lake to yourself, so bring your canoe or kayak—and enjoy. See *Camping the North Shore,* by Andrew Slade.

Camping and hiking: the perfect North Shore combination

Make the wild North Shore your destination for a week or weekend of hiking. Set up your tent or RV in a great campground and hike right from your campsite.

North Shore state parks well suited for combination car camping and hiking are

The Superior Hiking Trail practically runs through the campground at Cascade River State Park (pictured).

Gooseberry Falls (Hike #16 and 17), **Tettegouche** (Hike #22 and 23), and **Cascade River** (Hike #38 and 39). Enjoy the loop hikes in this book, take a hot shower afterwards, and end your day with s'mores around the campfire.

In addition, three shorter hikes around inland lakes are found in the Superior National Forest along Forest Road 172. Within about ten miles of each other are **Eighteen Lake** (Hike #26), **Divide Lake** (Hike #27) and **Hogback Lake** (Hike #28). Each one has a small campground right at the trailhead. Camp at one and hike all three trails.

These campgrounds—with detailed information on over 50 additional North Shore campgrounds, are featured in *Camping the North Shore*, by Andrew Slade.

The Superior National Forest

National forests are known as "the land of many uses." The Superior National Forest is indeed that, providing wilderness, ecological management, recreation and timber products. It's named after Lake Superior, even though only a small amount of the National Forest actually touches the big lake.

The Superior National Forest is nearly 4 million acres in size, and spreads from the North Shore to Voyageurs National Park and from the Iron Range to the Arrowhead Trail. You'll find over 400 miles of hiking, ranging from long-distance wilderness backpacking trails to short and sweet interpretive trails.

Eighteen of the 50 trails in this book are in the Superior National Forest. The very first sections of the Superior Hiking Trail were built by the Superior National Forest on its land in the Tofte and Lutsen area. The Kekekabic Trail and Border Route Trail both rely heavily on the National Forest.

In the core of the Forest is the Boundary Waters Canoe Area Wilderness. This is the largest federal wilderness east of the Rockies and north of the Everglades. Special rules and permits apply here, such as a maximum group size of 9 and no cans or bottles allowed. **Eagle Mountain** (Hike #41) and **Caribou Rock Trail** (Hike #42) both enter the BWCA.

27 Divide Lake

A 2.1 mile loop hike in the Superior National Forest near Isabella

You'll hike right on top of Minnesota's continental divide near the end of this loop.

▶ **What makes it unique.** At 1,938 feet in elevation, this is one of the highest lakes in Minnesota.

▶ **Finding the trailhead.** From the town of Finland, take Highway 1 north 16.1 miles to Isabella. Turn right on Forest Road 172 (Wanless Road) 4.8 miles to Divide Lake recreation area on right. Park at marked parking area, found in the middle of the small Superior National Forest campground.

Welcome to the top of the world. Hike around a quiet lake at the crest of the Laurentian Divide. Divide Lake is the headwaters of the mighty Manitou River. Camp here, bring a canoe and a fishing pole, and you can have a complete North Woods vacation.

It's the perfect complement to the Eighteen Lake trail (Hike #26) and Hogback Lake trail (Hike #28). You could go either direction around the lake; the description here is for the counter-clockwise direction.

The trail starts right from the small campground. As you hike, keep an eye out for log and stone cribbing. It appears that the lake was created or enhanced by earthen dams, perhaps to assist with moving timber during the major logging era of the early 20th century.

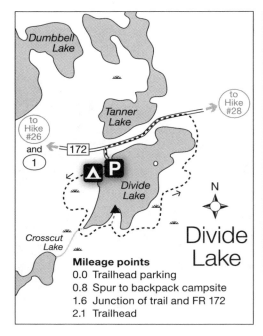

Distance: 2.1 miles

Time: 45 to 90 minutes

Difficulty: easy. The trail is well-maintained and level.

More info:
Superior National Forest,
Tofte District (218) 663-8060
tofte@fs.fed.us
McKenzie Map 204:
Dumbbell and Balsam Lakes

GPS coordinates:
N47° 36.60'
W091° 15.38'

Trailhead facilities: Vault toilet, campground, drinking water.

Mileage points
0.0 Trailhead parking
0.8 Spur to backpack campsite
1.6 Junction of trail and FR 172
2.1 Trailhead

Divide Lake is a designated trout lake. The water from here flows into Lake Superior and the Atlantic Ocean. Tanner Lake, on the other side of Forest Road 172, feeds the Kawishiwi River, which eventually leads to Hudson Bay.

About a third of the way around is a 150-yard spur trail leading to a backpack campsite. The campsite has a picnic table, latrine and a fire pit and is on a peninsula sticking out in the lake.

The trail is kept clear and wide. In addition to the earthen dams, the trail also crosses many small footbridges over creeks that drain Divide Lake into the Manitou River. Imagine this water cascading downstream all the way through the deep gorge and cascades of Crosby Manitou State Park (Hike #29).

The trail on the east side of the lake climbs up and down a bit more than on the west. It also enters mature birch and spruce forest. The soil is richer, making for easier walking. The last half mile is along Forest Road 172, with good views into the lakes on both sides of the continental divide and a bench down by the Divide lakeshore for angling or just relaxing.

❱ **Other options for this hike.** Bring a canoe, split your party up, and have one group paddle to the campsite. Then you can switch around hiking and paddling.

28 Hogback Lake

A 3.1 mile loop hike in the Superior National Forest north of Finland

The trail finishes with a scenic stretch along the north shore of Hogback Lake.

▶ **What makes it unique.** This is a well-maintained trail system in a near-wilderness environment, with trout fishing and remote campsites.

▶ **Finding the trailhead.** From Finland, take County Road 7 (Cramer Road) 23.4 miles north and east. Turn left on Forest Road 172 (Wanless Road). Watch for entrance 0.9 miles ahead on left, signed Hogback Lake Recreation Site. The trailhead is in a small picnic area between the campsites and the boat landing.

This landscape is full of lakes. And hills. Expect to wind around four different lakes and climb up and over countless hills.

Hogback Lake is where the trail starts, but on this route you'll spend a lot more time with Scarp Lake. It's beautiful country and a very pleasant surprise in the middle of a remote part of the Superior National Forest.

Geologically, a "hogback" is a steep-sided ridgeline, and the name of Hogback Lake probably refers to the steep ridgeline that forms the south shore of the lake.

This route takes you counterclockwise around Scarp Lake. Pack up a lunch to enjoy at a quiet lakeshore bench or campsite. The lakes are stocked with rainbow trout and splake.

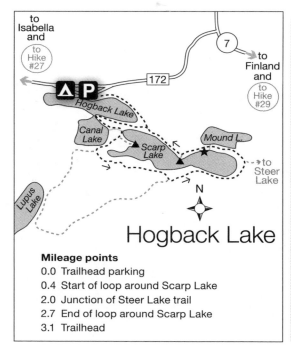

Hogback Lake

Mileage points

0.0 Trailhead parking
0.4 Start of loop around Scarp Lake
2.0 Junction of Steer Lake trail
2.7 End of loop around Scarp Lake
3.1 Trailhead

to Isabella and

to Hike #27

to Finland and

to Hike #29

to Steer Lake

Nearby Eats, Treats & Lodging

You can camp right at Hogback Lake in a Superior National Forest rustic campground. The campsites are so-so, but you can cook your meals right on the shore of the lake, and the price is right: the camping is free.

▮ You are just 5 miles by road from the Trestle Inn, on the Cramer Road. After your hike, stop in for a burger and a beverage.

Before taking off on the trail, visit the fishing pier to get a sense of the country. Note the steep terrain around the lake and the unusually clear water. If you look straight across the lake, you'll see a break in the shoreline that is the connection with Canal Lake. You will be at that point shortly.

From the trailhead parking area, you'll find a short trail along the shoreline to the boat landing. The trail continues along the shoreline of Hogback Lake, and then climbs away to the first of many ridgelines. Here you'll find the start of the loop around Scarp Lake. Stay right, hike straight down the spine of the hogback, and you'll soon be back down to Hogback Lake and the connecting channel to Canal Lake.

The trail cuts away from Canal Lake along a wet portage to Scarp Lake, and then climbs through deep forest. If you're ready for a break, take the 150-yard trail to the campsite, which sits out on a gravelly point on Scarp Lake. There's a wilderness latrine, picnic table and a fire pit.

Continue around Scarp Lake, and you'll learn about escarpments—the steep cliffs on the south side of the lake. Pass two junctions that are the ends of a loop to Lupus Lake.

Halfway around the lake, watch for an old wooden survey monument to the

Distance: 3.1 miles

Time: 1.5 to 2 hours

Difficulty: moderate. The trail is well maintained and well marked, though there is some steep terrain.

More info:
Tofte Ranger District
(218) 663-8060
www.fs.usda.gov/superior

GPS coordinates:
N47° 38.65'
W091° 08.15'

Trailhead facilities: Vault toilet, campground, picnic area, boat landing.

(Right, top) Hikers can stop at one of two campsites on Scarp Lake for lunch or an overnight experience; signs point the way at each intersection (bottom).

left of the trail. A longer level stretch takes you along the top of the escarpment.

At the east end of Scarp Lake, the trail has a short and very steep climb. You'll pass another trail junction, this one to Steer Lake and County Road 7. There's a lakeshore bench with a great view about 200 yards past the junction, alongside a creek flowing from Scarp Lake to little Mound Lake. Stop here for a rest, or continue another quarter-mile to the lakeshore campsite.

The trail continues along the top of the hogback ridgeline and completes the loop soon after the campsite.

▶ **Other options for this hike.** The loop around Scarp Lake has trails leading off to other lakes. Add an extra mile to your hike with the loop to Lupus Lake. The Minnesota DNR says, "Lupus Lake probably would provide anglers with plenty of action for small northern pike in a wild, uncrowded setting."

29 Humpback Trail

A 2.5 mile loop hike in Crosby Manitou State Park near Finland

State Park Hiking Club TRAIL

The Humpback Trail runs over four hard-rock humps, each with wide views atop.

▶ **What makes it unique.** Enjoy the highlights of this hiker's park on a diverse 2.5-mile loop.

▶ **Finding the trailhead.** Heading northeast from Finland on Highway 1, turn east on County Road 7 (Cramer Road). Follow Cramer Road 7.5 miles to park entrance on Bensen Lake Road. Follow Bensen Lake Road 0.5 miles to trailhead parking on the left, stopping if necessary at the registration station to buy a vehicle permit.

▶ **State park vehicle permit required;** at self-serve station on entrance road.

It's a wilderness gem just a few miles from the North Shore. George H. Crosby Manitou State Park is a hiker's park, since the only real development here is the extensive trail system. This hike combines three park hiking trails: the Humpback Trail, parts of the River Trail and the Middle Trail. It is best taken clockwise, to complete the more difficult section first.

There are four different overlapping loops that leave from the parking lot. If you like this hike, do one of the other loops on another day. This trail is the park's Hiking Club Trail, so keep an eye out for the geology-related password.

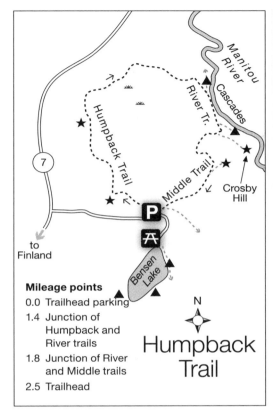

Mileage points

0.0 Trailhead parking
1.4 Junction of Humpback and River trails
1.8 Junction of River and Middle trails
2.5 Trailhead

N

Humpback Trail

Distance: 2.5 miles

Time: 1 to 2 hours

Difficulty: moderate. The first two parts of the loop (Humpback Trail and River Trail) have steep ups and downs and rough trail. The homestretch up the Middle Trail is smoother.

More info:
Tettegouche State Park
(218) 353-8800
www.dnr.state.mn.us/
state_parks/tettegouche
Map at trailhead and at
Tettegouche State Park
or McKenzie Map 103:
Taconite Harbor

GPS coordinates:
N47° 28.73'
W091° 06.72'

Trailhead facilities: Vault
toilet, drinking water (by
registration station).

The Humpback Trail leaves from the far left corner of the trailhead parking lot. The trail climbs up and over four different bedrock knobs (the so-called "humpbacks") on its way to the Manitou River. These knobs have great views to the west. The last of the four knobs is the hardest to climb up and over.

If you're familiar with North Shore geology, you may have heard that the rocks are mostly basalt, with rhyolite showing up from time to time. The bedrock along this trail is neither basalt nor rhyolite, but something in between: diorite. The first humpback is composed of monzodiorite, which geologist Ron Morton calls "Rotten Rock." The last three humpbacks are formed of ferrodiorite. These are all erosion-resistant rocks that—after millions of years of glaciers, wind and ice—stick up above the surrounding terrain.

The route descends to the Manitou River and meets the River Trail, which parallels the cascading river for nearly five miles. It's difficult hiking, with lots of ups and downs along slippery riverbank. When you hear the rush of water, step off the trail for a few yards to take in the Cascades, where the Manitou rages down a series of steps.

After getting a brief taste of the River Trail, you'll head up the Middle Trail. It's a steep climb up and out of the river valley, and then the trail levels off. There are two side trails to overlooks: the first goes left up to Crosby Hill and a river view; the second, about a half mile up, goes just 150 yards to an overlook down the valley to Lake Superior. Close to the end of the loop you'll see the perfect glacial erratic—a large diabase boulder left behind by the glacier.

▶ **Other options for this hike.** If you want a bit more hiking today, especially along the dramatic Manitou River, follow the River Trail past the Middle Trail to the Misquah and Yellow Birch trails, and use that trail to complete a loop of 3.5 miles. You won't miss the Hiking Club password if you do this.

Explore George H. Crosby Manitou State Park

If you think all state parks have fancy visitor centers, hot showers and interpretive exhibits, you'll be in for a surprise at George H. Crosby Manitou State Park. No showers or exhibits here; it's a remote, undeveloped wilderness park that's perfect for hikers.

Manitou is the third largest park on the North Shore, yet it is by far the least visited. Given its size and the number of visitors, it's literally 100 times less crowded here than at Gooseberry Falls State Park. There are more hiking trails than any other park in the area except Jay Cooke State Park.

The park straddles the deep and rugged gorge of the Manitou River. "Manitou" is the Ojibwe word for "spirit," and you can definitely feel the spirit in this park. The park scatters 21 backcountry campsites throughout the gorge area and around the shores of Bensen Lake.

Benson Lake is a quiet gem with a small picnic area. An easy boardwalk trail, less than one mile long, circles the lake.

Crosby Manitou is managed by Tettegouche State Park, and you can stop at the Tettegouche office on Highway 61 for the latest information on trail closures, etc.

30 Caribou Falls

A 1.3 mile in-and-out hike on the Superior Hiking Trail near Little Marais

Reach gorgeous Caribou Falls with an easy hike that invites exploration of the Caribou River along the way.

▶ **What makes it unique.** Get up close and personal with a rugged North Shore river, from its bubbling rapids past a gorgeous waterfall to a picnic-worthy overlook and remote-feeling footbridge. The access from Highway 61 is as easy as it gets.

▶ **Finding the trailhead.** Trailhead parking is directly off Highway 61 between Little Marais and Schroeder at mile marker 70.5.

This highway pull-off was once a full-fledged state park. While there's been a trail up to Caribou Falls for many decades, the opening of the Superior Hiking Trail here in the late 1980s turned what had been a rugged riverbank for anglers into a wide and clear trail that's safe for all ages.

It's a short hike to the falls and bridge, but if you take your time and investigate the many stopping points along the way, you can enjoy a full two or three hours along the Caribou River.

From the parking lot, the trail to the falls starts by the vault toilet. This is a spur of the Superior Hiking Trail, so you can follow white blazes. For the first 200 yards or so, the trail parallels the Caribou River. There are little pull-offs where you can sit on a rock and enjoy the river.

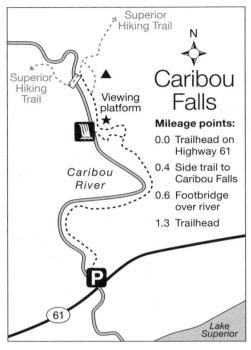

Superior
Hiking Trail

Superior
Hiking
Trail

▲

Viewing
platform

★

Caribou
Falls

N

Distance: 1.3 miles

Time: 1 to 2 hours

Difficulty: easy. The trail is
wide and forgiving and the
climbs are mild.

More info:
Superior Hiking Trail Assn.
www.superiorhiking.org
(218) 834-2700
Map Series D

GPS coordinates:
N47° 27.90'
W091° 01.82'

Trailhead facilities: vault
toilet

Mileage points:

0.0 Trailhead on
    Highway 61

0.4 Side trail to
    Caribou Falls

0.6 Footbridge
    over river

1.3 Trailhead

*Caribou
River*

P

61

*Lake
Superior*

The trail climbs from the
riverbank and at about one-
quarter mile reaches the top
of the Caribou River gorge.
Through birch and spruce
trees, views open up of the river valley and Lake Superior.

There's a major unmarked intersection at 0.4 miles in. Take the left hand
trail and within a few yards you're on well-built stairs that descend a steep slope
down into the gorge of Caribou Falls. After some dramatic cliff-side twists and
turns, the stairs end right at the edge of the pool below the falls. Depending on
the year and the flow of the river, you might find a gravel beach here or the steps
might just end over the water. Take a nice long break to look around this natural
amphitheater.

At low water, walk up the Caribou River to the falls.

Back up on the main
trail, the SHT spur climbs
up and leads through
a grove of tall old white
pine trees before reaching
a multilevel viewing platform. The platform hangs
over the upper gorge of the
Caribou River, which is so
deep you can only hear the

rushing water, not see it. You could have a picnic for twenty people on the large platform and it wouldn't be crowded. The view back down the river toward Lake Superior is beautiful.

Just upstream from the viewing platform is a SHT campsite and then the footbridge over the Caribou River gorge. The gorge here is deep, but from the footbridge you can see the torrents both upstream and down. Stop and check out the entries in the SHT trail register by the footbridge, or just sit on the conveniently located bench.

When you've had your fill of the rugged Caribou, return the way you came.

Bring the whole family to the deck above Caribou Falls.

▶ **Other options for this hike.** On a hot day in July or August, if the water level is down, put on your water sandals, grab a hiking pole, and follow the river bed all the way from the highway to the waterfall. Then you can return to the trailhead on the safe hiking trail.

Sugarloaf Cove

Sugarloaf Cove, on the lakeshore at mile marker 73.3, is a great spot to explore and relax for a few hours. It looks and feels like another state park, but is actually owned and management by a nonprofit association.

A one-mile interpretive trail starts at the parking lot. Pick up the detailed booklet and head out; you'll learn about the history of log rafting on the site, the world-class examples of Precambrian lava flows, and the native forest restoration work evident throughout. The trail runs through a pine plantation, above a rocky shoreline, then down a cobblestone beach and finally up little Sugarloaf Creek.

The trail ends at the interpretive center, a beautiful log building with exhibits and a small reading area. Be sure to check out the historic pictures of what the Cove looked like when it was a log rafting site for Consolidated Paper.

31 Temperance River

A 2.6 mile loop hike in Temperance River State Park near Tofte

The Temperance River cascades to its deep gorge. This hike leads to the best view-points.

▶ **What makes it unique.** There is nothing like the dramatic gorge of the Temperance River. Nowhere else on the North Shore has a river cut so deep and yet has remained so accessible.

▶ **Finding the trailhead.** Trailhead is directly off Highway 61 just east of the Temperance River bridge at mile marker 80.3.

The Temperance River gorge is amazing. You could easily spend an entire hour looking down into the gorge, tracing its potholes and hidden waterfalls, exploring above and below Highway 61. Completing this hike (and earning your Hiking Club Trail miles) gets you a bonus: the wide and scenic upper Temperance River valley.

The trail begins from the northeast parking lot along Highway 61. It's labeled as the Hiking Club Trail and also as a Superior Hiking Trail spur trail. The trail is wide and paved for the first 100 yards down to a viewing platform. Stop at the viewing platform and peer deep into the dark gorge of the Temperance River.

The Temperance has large lakes in its headwaters that moderate the flow,

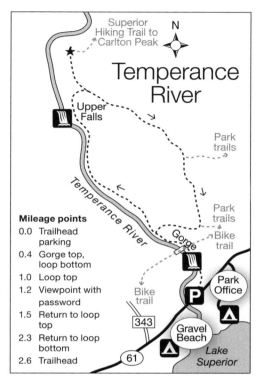

Superior
Hiking Trail to
Carlton Peak

N

Temperance
River

Upper
Falls

Park
trails

Park
trails

Mileage points

0.0	Trailhead parking
0.4	Gorge top, loop bottom
1.0	Loop top
1.2	Viewpoint with password
1.5	Return to loop top
2.3	Return to loop bottom
2.6	Trailhead

Bike trail

Bike trail

343

P Park Office

Gravel Beach

61

Lake Superior

Distance: 2.6 miles

Time: 1 to 2 hours

Difficulty: easy. Wide trails and plenty of safety walls make this a trail for all ages and abilities.

More info:
Temperance River State Park
(218) 663-3100
www.dnr.state.mn.us/state_parks/temperance_river

GPS coordinates:
N47° 33.30'
W090° 52.42'

Trailhead facilities: Vault toilet, campground.

so water rushes through the gorge year-round. The gorge is cut into what appears to be one massive basalt lava flow.

Take your time exploring the gorge, including all the overlooks. One of the best views is from the bike trail that crosses the gorge about halfway up. After a third of a mile, the gorge suddenly ends and you see the wide and shallow upper Temperance River. One writer refers to this as the calm Dr. Jekyll to the gorge's wild Mr. Hyde.

The route runs right alongside the river for the next quarter mile, then climbs slowly uphill before leaving the river completely. If you'd enjoy another waterfall experience, you can follow an unmarked spur trail down toward the river and Upper Falls.

This route is a modified lollipop-shaped loop, with a stick at both ends and a loop in the middle. The far stick leads 300 yards to a view of the river valley.

The route continues clockwise around the main loop and follows a wide, former XC ski trail. It continues for almost a mile past three intersections through a dead and dying birch forest. The route always bears right; look for, but don't count on finding, the faded Hiking Club Trail signs. Take time to notice flowers and mushrooms underfoot.

The loop brings you back to the Temperance River just above the gorge, and you can find more great views on your way back to the trailhead.

▶ **Other options for this hike.** This is also the trailhead for the popular and challenging climb to Carlton Peak. The hike to the summit is 3.5 miles one-way and 900 vertical feet of climbing.

Nearby **Eats, Treats & Lodging**

The Temperance River State Park campground makes an excellent base camp for this hike and the hike to Carlton Peak. After your hike, visit the lovely cobblestone beach at the park's picnic area. ▮ Your hike ends very close to Tofte and its classy restaurants and stores.

Explore Temperance River State Park

BEST NORTH SHORE

Legend has it that the Temperance River got its name because it had no "bar" at its mouth. If you visit other North Shore rivers, you'll see that most, but not all, have a gravel beach running across from the cliff on one side of the river to the cliff on the other side. But if you take the time to explore the state park, especially its delightful shoreline, you'll find that there is in fact a bar at the mouth now. Maybe we should rename the river?

"Temperance" means moderation. This is not a moderate state park. Sure it's small, at 539 acres. Still, you can make the greatest climb on the entire Superior Hiking Trail from your lakeshore campsite to the top of Carlton Peak, over 900 feet in 3 miles. You can explore the North Shore's deepest, darkest crevice along the Gorge Trail. Or you can look for the North Shore's unusual coastal wildflowers, such as the carnivorous butterwort, in the cracks of the expansive shoreline rocks.

Temperance could have been the site of the North Shore's largest dam, if plans from 1913 had gone forward. Fletcher Brothers of Minneapolis owned the rights to develop a 60 megawatt electric plant for lighting up Tofte.

With your state park permit, you can visit or camp by one of the North Shore's best gravel beaches. The park's picnic area, in the lower campground, has a wide and accessible beach that tempts swimmers, especially when the river is running well and a huge eddy circles around. But use caution: the Temperance River gorge has had more drowning fatalities (nine between 1983 and 2009) than any other North Shore state park.

With your state park vehicle permit, you can enjoy the easy-to-reach beach at the Temperance River State picnic area.

32 Carlton Peak

A 3.2 mile out-and-back hike on the Superior Hiking Trail near Tofte

From the top of Carlton Peak, the Lake Superior views are astounding.

▶ **What makes it unique.** This is the easy way up Carlton Peak, and gets you to one of the most scenic places on the North Shore, if not all of Minnesota.

▶ **Finding the trailhead.** From mile marker 82.9 on Highway 61 (downtown Tofte), turn north on County Road 2 (Sawbill Trail). Take the Sawbill Trail 2.5 miles inland to Britton Peak Trailhead on the right.

Take the easy way up Carlton Peak, one of the North Shore's most dramatic high points. The climb up is only 360 vertical feet. (If you hiked in to Carlton Peak from Highway 61 by the Temperance River instead, you'd climb 900 feet.)

Carlton Peak was named after Reuben B. Carlton, an early promoter of North Shore copper mining. The peak was owned by 3M and prospected for corundum, one of the hardest minerals known. In 1907, a crew opened a six-foot wide tunnel. Like 3M's original mine in what is now Tettegouche State Park, this mine did not produce corundum. Eventually, 3M gave the land to the State of Minnesota via The Nature Conservancy. It is now part of Temperance River State Park.

Find the Carlton Peak trail at the far end of the Britton Peak parking lot. The trail crosses County Road 2 right away, then goes slightly downhill for over a half mile through scrubby young forest. The real climb to the Peak starts at about two-thirds of a mile.

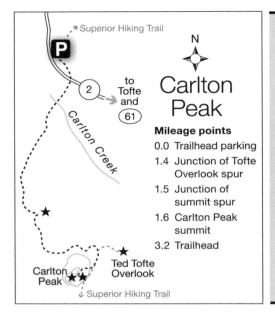

Superior Hiking Trail

N

to Tofte and 61

Carlton Peak

Carlton Creek

Ted Tofte Overlook

Carlton Peak

Superior Hiking Trail

Mileage points
0.0 Trailhead parking
1.4 Junction of Tofte Overlook spur
1.5 Junction of summit spur
1.6 Carlton Peak summit
3.2 Trailhead

Distance: 3.2 miles

Time: 1 to 2 hours

Difficulty: moderate. It's a long but gradual climb to the rocky summit.

More info:
Superior Hiking Trail Assn.
www.superiorhiking.org
(218) 834-2700
Map Series E or McKenzie
Map 102: Lutsen, Tofte

GPS coordinates:
N47° 35.91'
W090° 51.70'

Trailhead facilities: Vault toilet

The trail runs below the north face of Carlton Peak. You may notice boreal wildflowers suited to the cold and dark of this side of the mountain, flowers such as twinflower and pyrola. The rocks are covered with moss, which will thrive on the north side of rocks just like it does on the north side of trees.

The 250-yard spur trail to the Ted Tofte Overlook is well worth exploring, due to the open rock mounds and big views of Lake Superior. You'll find a plaque commemorating Jason Robert Feltl, who died in a climbing accident on Carlton Peak in 1989.

Just past the spur to the Ted Tofte Overlook is the spur to the main summit of Carlton Peak. It's a short scamper up bare rock and past jack pine trees to the expansive open summit. Look for the remains of a fire tower. There are often groups of people lingering at the summit, but you can easily find your own private nook. The view extends far up and down the shore.

Nearby **Eats, Treats & Lodging**

The Coho Café in Tofte has fine foods in an informal setting. ∎ If it's a pleasant day, grab picnic foods at the North Shore Market and wrap up your day at the cobblestone beach in Temperance River State Park. ∎ For more info, visit **www.visitcookcounty.com**.

After fully enjoying the summit, head back down to the main trail and record your observations and feelings at the trail register. Then return back to County Road 2 by retracing your steps.

▶ **Other options for this hike.** Many people continue on the Superior Hiking Trail to Highway 61 at the Temperance River for a 4.8-mile hike. You can easily use the Superior Hiking Shuttle to help with this (meet them at the Temperance River parking lot and ride to the Britton Peak Trailhead). You can also hike to Carlton Peak round trip from Highway 61. That's a 7-mile round trip hike with a much higher climb (see Hike #31).

Hard rocks and high points: "anorthosite" is for climbers

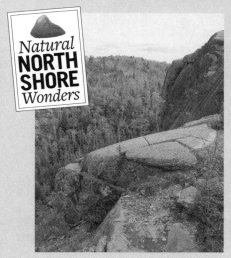

Natural **NORTH SHORE** *Wonders*

After a billion years of erosion from wind, water and glaciers, the highest points in the North Shore landscape are often the hardest and most resistant to erosion. In the central North Shore, those hard, high points are often composed of a rock called **anorthosite**.

Many of the best overlooks in the central North Shore, from Corundum Point in Split Rock Lighthouse State Park (Hike #19) to Carlton Peak (Hike #32), sit atop massive blocks of anorthosite. Chunks of anorthosite were carried from deep within the earth by diabase magma flowing toward the surface during the great Midcontinent Rift era 1.1 billion years ago. The rock is so hard that the nascent Minnesota Mining and Manufacturing considered making sandpaper out of it.

Anorthosite overlooks are recognized by the light-colored rock that weathers into smooth and rounded surfaces. But the surface only looks smooth. Rock climbers who have flocked to these same outcrops for decades know otherwise. "Jamming in anorthosite is a little like sticking your hand into an industrial grinder," writes Dave Pagel in *Superior Climbs*. "What bites the hand usually delights the feet; the fractioning properties of this rock are unparalleled."

Other well-known anorthosite viewpoints are Mt. Trudee, Section 13 (Hike #25) and Britton Peak.

33 Leveaux Mountain

A 3.2 mile loop hike on the Superior Hiking Trail, near Tofte

Viewed from Oberg Mountain, Leveaux Mountain shows its steep inland side, the back side of a classic sawtooth mountain.

▶ **What makes it unique.** Combine great natural history with great views for a classic North Shore hike.

▶ **Finding the trailhead.** From mile marker 87.4 on Highway 61, take Forest Road 336 (Onion River Road) 2.1 miles to large, well-marked parking area on left. Both the Leveaux Mountain and Oberg Mountain trails start from this lot. For the Leveaux hike, park at the far end of the lot and look for the sign.

This hike is adjacent to the Oberg Mountain hike. Why choose this one? This hike is a bit more challenging and also much less crowded.

If the North Shore does in fact have mountains, Leveaux Mountain is a classic. Leveaux is a great example of a sawtooth mountain. It rises gradually from the shore, but drops off steeply on the back. Put six or eight of these mountains in a row and you get a pattern like the teeth along the edge of a saw. Or maybe like baby cows lying in a field; "Le veaux" is French for "the calves."

This hike is made of one straight section of trail and two short loops. The first loop climbs up to the top of Leveaux Mountain. The second, shorter loop leads to a great view of Lake Superior and Carlton Peak.

The hike to Leveaux has great examples of North Shore natural history. The

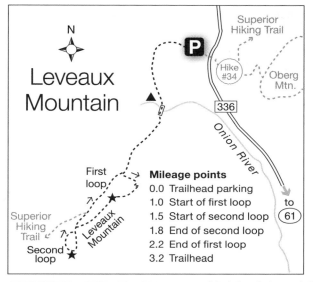

trail starts with almost a mile of spruce, birch and fir forest. This is considered boreal forest. Then the trail starts to climb and the forest changes to sugar maple—a northern hardwood forest.

The first loop starts at about one mile in; hike clockwise around the loop. This gets you to big inland views right away.

The trail climbs with switchbacks right up the steep edge of Leveaux. Do not miss the one great inland overlook on the right side about 200 yards from the top of the switchbacks. This view is especially scenic.

At the far end of the first loop, the trail leads just 50 yards to the start of the second loop. This junction may not be marked; watch carefully. Going either direction is fine. The view is tremendous. You can see forever down the shore toward Silver Bay. Taconite Harbor is obvious on the lakeshore, and Carlton Peak is the big dark lump on the right.

After completing the second loop, you'll return to complete the first one. You reconnect with the main Superior Hiking Trail on the way back. Watch for a massive talus slope up to your right. Above those scrambled boulders is a cliff. On top of that cliff is the big inland overlook you were at less than an hour ago.

Distance: 3.2 miles

Time: 1.5 to 2.5 hours

Difficulty: moderate. The trail is wide and in very good condition. There's a challenging climb up the steep side of Leveaux Mountain.

More info:
Superior Hiking Trail Assn.
www.superiorhiking.org
(218) 834-2700
Map Series E or McKenzie Map 102: Lutsen, Tofte

GPS coordinates:
N47° 37.69'
W090° 47.09'

Trailhead facilities: Vault toilet, warming shack.

▶ Other options for this hike. Combine this hike with the Oberg Mountain trail (Hike #34) for a great day of hiking. Both hikes start and end from the same parking lot.

Hard rocks and high points: "Sawtooth" is scenic

Looking down the North Shore, the Sawtooth formation is easy to see from Artist's Point and the Grand Marais harbor.

The North Shore's best-known geologic formation may be the **Sawtooth Mountains.** Five mountains, from Leveaux to Lookout, appear from the distance like the teeth of a saw, rising gradually from the lake and descending steeply away from the lake. You can see the formation really well looking west from Artist's Point in Grand Marais. It's commemorated on the logo of the Superior Hiking Trail and the term "Sawtooth" is used for the elementary school in Grand Marais, as well as the clinic, a lumber store, a motel and a chiropractor.

Natural **NORTH SHORE** *Wonders*

During the Midcontinent Rift era, layers and layers of igneous rock piled on top of each other. Later, the layers tilted into what is now Lake Superior, at about a 20-degree angle. Erosion removed much of the rock, but left the harder rock. The long, gradual side of each of the Sawtooth Mountains, rising from Lake Superior, is all one lava flow, a harder type of basalt known as "porphyry." Two main lava flows make up the Sawtooth Mountains: the Leveaux Porphyry and the Terrace Point Flow.

Sawtooth Mountain hikes in this book that reach great tooth-edge views are: Leveaux Mountain (Hike #33), Lutsen Gondola Hike (Hike #35), Caribou Trail to Lutsen (Hike #36), Caribou Trail to Cascade (Hike #37) and Lookout Mountain (Hike #38). At each hike, watch for the dramatic inland cliff edge falling away from the ridge; you're looking right down the thick end of a billion-year-old lava flow.

34 Oberg Mountain

A 2.2 mile loop hike on the Superior Hiking Trail near Tofte

Chloe and Andrew enjoy the view of Oberg Lake and the tapestry of fall colors below. This is the last of the seven overlooks on the summit.

❱ What makes it unique. Easy access to dramatic viewpoints makes this a terrific beginner's hike with big scenic payoffs. It is spectacular during fall colors.

❱ Finding the trailhead. From mile marker 87.4 on Highway 61, take Forest Road 336 (Onion River Road) 2.1 miles to large, well-marked parking area on left. Both the Leveaux Mountain and Oberg Mountain trails start from this lot. For the Oberg hike, park at the close end of the lot and look for the sign.

This is one of the most popular hikes on the North Shore, and for good reason. With just enough hiking to break a sweat and earn a granola bar, you can enjoy seven fantastic viewpoints of Lake Superior and rugged inland ridges. The maple forests come alive each fall like a tapestry of autumn.

Because of its popularity, this hike does not provide much solitude. On fall color weekends, come early in the day or late in the afternoon. You can still find your favorite overlook and tuck yourself away somewhere for a few long minutes to ponder the lake and landscape in solitude.

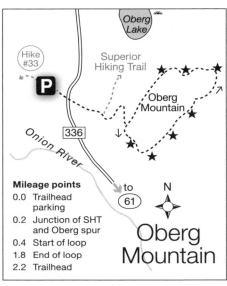

Distance: 2.2 miles

Time: 1 to 2 hours

Difficulty: easy. With just a moderate climb, this trail is wide and well-marked.

More info:
Superior Hiking Trail Assn.
www.superiorhiking.org
(218) 834-2700
Map Series E or McKenzie Map 102: Lutsen, Tofte

GPS coordinates:
N47° 37.69'
W090° 47.09'

Trailhead facilities: Vault toilet, warming shack.

From the trailhead, the wide and easy trail climbs gradually past massive white cedar trees. This is the main Superior Hiking Trail, but after less than a quarter mile you'll turn off on the Oberg Loop to the right. It's a steady climb of 200 feet in elevation, using big switchbacks to climb up into the sugar maple forest that caps off Oberg.

In less than a half mile, the real fun starts. You'll pass by the junction of the 1.4-mile summit loop. Most people hike this counterclockwise. It's best to go with the flow: if you go clockwise, you'd constantly pass people going the other direction.

There are seven viewpoints scattered along the next mile of trail. Between viewpoints, the trail runs through mature maple forest, providing spectacular color in the fall season. In fact, the cover photo of this book was taken along this trail.

The first overlook takes in the dramatic shape of Leveaux Mountain. At the second overlook, take a break on the log bench and look for the Apostle Islands straight across the blue expanse of Lake Superior.

At the third overlook, walk out to the edge of the rock for a 120-degree view of the open Lake. The big view of Lake Superior continues for another 100 yards or so, with views opening up toward the coastal village of Grand Marais.

The fifth overlook is one of the most popular for group photographs. A good Samaritan could stand here for an hour and offer to take pictures. A railing keeps you from falling over the edge and frames the view of Lutsen's Moose Mountain and the Lake Superior shoreline.

The sixth overlook is for artists, providing a small view of Oberg Lake framed by a steep cliff. The view of Oberg Lake and the forest below is much better at the seventh and last overlook.

It's just under a half mile through maple woods back to the start of the loop, then it's back down the hill to the trailhead.

▶ **Other options for this hike.** Combine this hike with Leveaux Mountain (Hike #33) for a great, full day of scenic North Shore hiking.

Chloe and Andrew walk along the fourth overlook (top); at the fifth overlook, the view stretches far up the North Shore (bottom).

35 Lutsen Gondola Hike

A 4.2 mile loop hike on the Superior Hiking Trail near Lutsen

Lutsen Mountain's gondolas give you a leisurely ride to the top edge of distant Moose Mountain. The last minute is a doozy as the gondola climbs the cliff.

▶ **What makes it unique.** Starting off with a ride on Lutsen's gondola, this hike is reminiscent of hikes in the Alps.

▶ **Finding the trailhead.** From Highway 61 mile marker 90.1, take County Road 5 (Ski Hill Road) 2.9 miles to base of gondola.

This is a very European hiking experience. The Lutsen Summit Express Gondola whisks you away to distant and dramatic Moose Mountain, where you can have a pre-hike snack at the chalet or on the deck. The first part of the trail is practically along the edge of Moose Mountain's sawtooth steep side, like a fixed mountaineering route through the Alps.

Do not underestimate the challenge of this hike. The gondola gives you about a 400-foot uphill advantage. Although you start with a downhill, you must still climb up and over Mystery Mountain.

Taking the gondola requires a one-way ticket (about $17 per person; get current prices and gondola hours of operation at www.lutsen.com). Tickets are available in the gift shop at the base of the gondola. The gondola operates daily from mid-June to mid-October, with extended weekend hours.

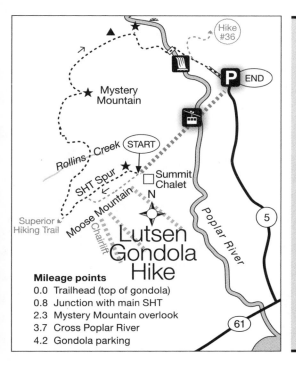

Mileage points
0.0 Trailhead (top of gondola)
0.8 Junction with main SHT
2.3 Mystery Mountain overlook
3.7 Cross Poplar River
4.2 Gondola parking

Distance: 4.2 miles

Time: 2 to 3 hours

Difficulty: moderate. Although the gondola ride gives you a slight uphill advantage, this trail has challenging terrain and a pretty big climb up and over Mystery Mountain.

More info:
Superior Hiking Trail Assn.
www.superiorhiking.org
(218) 834-2700
Map Series E or McKenzie Map 102: Lutsen, Tofte

GPS coordinates:
N 47° 39.85'
W090° 42.86'

Trailhead facilities:
Restrooms, drinking water, gift shop, restaurant.

The gondola ride is a real treat as you make a dramatic climb up the cliff face of Moose Mountain.

At the top is the Summit Chalet. Enjoy the restaurant or just the expansive views from the deck of the far shore toward Grand Marais.

Begin your hike right by the gondola exit. You'll follow an array of signs leading to the "Observation Deck," "Hiking Trails," and for the Superior Hiking Trail. After 150 feet, you'll come to a junction; your trail is on the right, toward the Observation Deck. Stop at the deck and preview your whole hiking route down into the Rollins Creek valley below, up and over Mystery Mountain straight ahead, then around to the base of the gondola.

From the observation deck, backtrack about 20 yards to the sign marking the Superior Hiking Trail spur trail and pointing to the left. This first part of the route is along an official Superior Hiking Trail spur, which leads to the main Superior Hiking Trail. Along the spur, look for the white paint blazes.

The spur trail runs right below the crest of Moose Mountain. Moose Mountain is a classic North Shore sawtooth mountain, and you are hiking just down from the tip of one of those saw teeth, on the steep side. The downhill ski runs are on the gentle side. The trail here is a real challenge as it dives through cracks in the cliff and alongside curvy white cedar trees.

After a half mile of cliff-edge fun, the trail finally heads downhill and meets up with the main Superior Hiking Trail. Turn right here. The trail descends steeply into the Rollins Creek valley, which is damp and full of ferns.

The hike up and over Mystery Mountain is a fascinating experience in forest ecology. You will find sugar maple trees everywhere. Big sugar maple trees create a green canopy. Medium sugar maple trees snake their way up looking for openings of sunlight. Even saplings, by the thousands, pretend to be wildflowers as they carpet the forest floor. Sugar maples are the old-growth forest here. Without a serious disturbance like a major forest fire, the maples will be replaced by more maple.

There aren't many viewpoints along Mystery Mountain, so enjoy the one big overlook you do get. You look back to the cliffs of Moose Mountain and get broad views of the Poplar River valley.

The trail descends to cross the Poplar River, with a dramatic downstream view of Upper

The trail scampers along the sawtooth edge of Moose Mountain.

Falls and the canyon. The trail here joins XC ski trails for the last half mile.

▶ **Other options for this hike.** Skip the challenging half mile of cliff-edge terrain at the beginning of this hike and enjoy panoramic Lake Superior fall color views by following the wide Lutsen "Ridgeline" ski run. Just past the third and last chair lift, a hiking and biking trail continues into the woods, connecting with the Superior Hiking Trail spur. Join the Superior Hiking Trail spur here and finish the entire Lutsen Gondola Hike as described above.

36 Caribou Trail to Lutsen

A 6.4 mile shuttle hike on the Superior Hiking Trail near Lutsen

From Hunters Rock, enjoy the view of untouched Lake Agnes.

▶ **What makes it unique.** This hike starts and ends up high in the North Shore ridgeline. Though it leads through rugged and beautiful country, the trail is relatively level.

▶ **Finding the trailhead.** From Highway 61 mile marker 92.0, take County Road 4 (Caribou Trail) 4.1 miles to trailhead parking on the right at White Sky Trail. The trailhead parking is shared with a public access to Caribou Lake.

This is an excellent hike in which to use a vehicle shuttle. Work with other hikers in your party or use the Superior Hiking Shuttle service to leave one car at the Lutsen Mountains trailhead (see Hike #35 for directions). Going east to west on this section of the Superior Hiking Trail gets you a height advantage, giving you about 150 vertical feet of extra downhill.

Overall, this section of trail is one of the flatter portions on the whole Superior Hiking Trail. There are steep climbs, but they're short. Despite the lack of climbing, the views are as dramatic as anywhere on the Superior Hiking Trail.

The first mile of this hike is marked with white paint blazes.

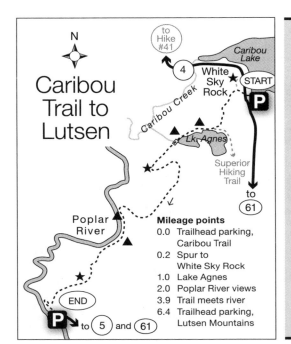

N

Caribou Trail to Lutsen

to Hike #41

4

White Sky Rock

START

Caribou Lake

P

Caribou Creek

Lk. Agnes

Superior Hiking Trail

to 61

Poplar River

Mileage points
0.0 Trailhead parking, Caribou Trail
0.2 Spur to White Sky Rock
1.0 Lake Agnes
2.0 Poplar River views
3.9 Trail meets river
6.4 Trailhead parking, Lutsen Mountains

END

P to 5 and 61

Distance: 6.4 miles

Time: 3 to 4 hours

Difficulty: moderate. There are a few steep climbs and some rough terrain, but this trail is great for the average hiker.

More info: Superior Hiking Trail Assn. www.superiorhiking.org (218) 834-2700 Map Series E or McKenzie Map 102: Lutsen, Tofte

GPS coordinates: N47° 42.43' W090° 40.04'

Trailhead facilities: None

A description of this route as relatively level might sound crazy as you start the hike from the Caribou Trail parking area. Cross County Road 4 and start climbing. You reach maple forest very quickly; on most Superior Hiking Trail sections, you have to climb up a good ways to get into the ridgeline maples.

Take the spur trail to White Sky Rock, an anorthosite knob. It's a short but steep 200 yards to a dramatic overlook of Caribou Lake and distant Lake Superior. White Sky was an Anishinaabe man and a close friend of the Nelson family that developed Lutsen Resort. He had a hunting shack in this area, and when White Sky passed away in 1913 from tuberculosis, Carl Nelson named this overlook after him. As Cathy Wurzer puts it in her book *Tales of the Road: Highway 61*, "Over the years, countless hikers have huffed and puffed their way up the steep cliff to White Sky Rock and been rewarded with the same panoramic view White Sky himself no doubt enjoyed."

After the White Sky Rock spur, the next half mile of trail runs through old-growth forest filled with massive boulders and wooded cliff edges. The trail engineering is remarkable, including two staircases carved out of solid logs.

Lake Agnes is a quiet scenic treat, right at the junction of the spur trail and the main Superior Hiking Trail. The trail follows the shore for a half mile, passing scenic campsites and has a great open view at Hunters Rock.

The Poplar River valley dominates the next four miles of trail. You'll come out of a thick maple forest at a very scenic overlook with the river winding through the valley below. Look off to the left and pick out the ridgeline above the river. You might be able to pick out the cellphone towers atop Lutsen's Eagle Mountain, very near the end of the trail. Yes, there is excellent reception here.

There are three big views of the Poplar River valley, and then the trail descends slightly to a long bottomland. The walking is a bit monotonous here, until all of a sudden you are right on the banks of the Poplar River itself. The trail runs riverside for a quarter of a mile, passing two campsites. After the campsites, it's a long climb into an upland maple forest. Watch for an open rocky area off to the right where you'll find a view back to the ridge you passed almost three miles earlier on your hike.

The last half mile of trail is a rather steep and rocky descent to the Poplar River. Here it's no longer the placid winding river you hiked along earlier. It's a cascading waterfall-ridden river caught in a steep rocky valley for its last run to Lake Superior.

The fungus among us

In the month before fall colors drape the North Shore forests in reds and oranges, the North Shore forest floor has its own explosion of color. The late-summer, early-fall

Natural NORTH SHORE Wonders

mushroom season, like the tree color season, depends strongly on weather conditions. The cooler and moister the late summer, the better the mushrooms will be.

Mushrooms pop up alongside hiking trails, either right out of the ground or out of rotting logs half buried already in the ground. Some of the more common North Shore fall mushrooms are the orange-colored **Fly Agaric** and the white-colored **Destroying Angel,** both of which are very poisonous.

You'll find **Chanterelles,** considered delicious by some, in the North Shore's pine and spruce forests.

Fascinating Fungi of the North Woods, by Larry Weber and Cora Mollen, has top-notch illustrations and natural history information—and it fits in your fanny pack.

37 Caribou Trail to Cascade

A 8.1 mile shuttle hike on the Superior Hiking Trail near Lutsen, Minnesota

Andrew checks out one of the many inland views from sawtooth ridges on this hike.

▶ **What makes it unique.** This through-hike along the dramatic crest of three Sawtooth Mountains ridgelines has far-reaching views, and finishes with a downhill run along the rushing Cascade River of Cascade River State Park.

▶ **Finding the trailhead.** The best way to plan this hike is with a shuttle that you meet at the Cascade River wayside rest (where you'll park your car), at mile marker 100 between Lutsen and Grand Marais. To reach the starting trailhead, from Highway 61 mile marker 92.0, take County Road 4 (Caribou Trail) 2.8 miles to County Road 39. Turn right on County Road 39 and travel 0.3 miles to the SHT crossing, clearly visible on the right side of the road. Both the Superior Hiking Shuttle and Harriet Quarles Transportation can provide this shuttle service.

This hike requires a shuttle. From west to east, it's a long gorgeous run along the edge of unnamed Sawtooth mountains, and for the finish it's a glorious downhill stroll along the waterfalls of the Cascade River. Park at the lovely wayside rest at the mouth of the Cascade River. From the parking lot, the Superior Hiking Shuttle will pick up your hiking group and drive the 15-minute drive up the Caribou Trail on Friday, Saturday, or Sunday (check their published schedule). Or, if you'd

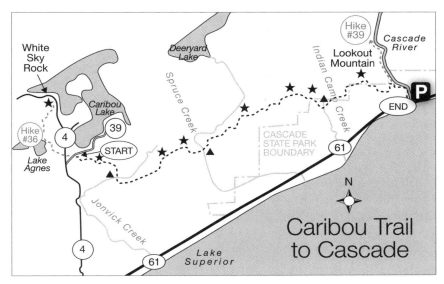

White
Sky
Rock

Deeryard
Lake

Hike
#39

Cascade
River

Lookout
Mountain

Caribou
Lake

Spruce Creek

Indian Camp Creek

END

Hike
#36

39

4

CASCADE
STATE PARK
BOUNDARY

P

Lake
Agnes

START

61

Jonvick Creek

4

61

Lake
Superior

N

Caribou Trail
to Cascade

Mileage points:

0.0 Trailhead on County Road 39
0.9 Jonvick Creek
2.8 Spruce Creek
5.8 Indian Camp Creek
6.8 Lookout Mountain
8.1 Cascade River wayside

Distance: 8.1 miles

Time: 4 to 6 hours

Difficulty: moderate. It's a long hike, and the first few miles are a slog when wet, but the climbs are forgiving.

More info:
Superior Hiking Trail Assn.
www.superiorhiking.org
(218) 834-2700
Map Series E

GPS coordinates:
N47° 41.69'
W090° 39.69'

Trailhead facilities: None

like to be more flexible with your departure time, arrange a shuttle with Harriet Quarles at a time convenient to you.

Parking is limited along County Road 39. If you need to leave a car at the Caribou Trail end of the hike (or if you're arranging your own shuttle with two cars), you might want to start at the official SHT trailhead on Caribou Lake and add 1.5 miles of the SHT past lovely Lake Agnes.

This hike starts high and goes higher. The trailhead is at 1400' above sea level, and the first quarter mile takes you even further up. It's private land at the start, and atop the first ridge, the trail goes right through a small amphitheater used by the local church camp Cathedral of the Pines. Enjoy the view of Caribou Lake from here. The forest is all sugar maple for nearly the first mile, and there are three or four more stretches of maple, making this a lovely, off-the-beaten path fall colors hike.

This hike traverses three Sawtooth mountain ridgelines—with a gradual slope on the Lake Superior side and a steep, cliff-like drop-off on the inland side.

If you don't like mud, time this hike for a dry season or a dry year. The first two miles are by far the lowest and wettest of the hike.

Jonvick Creek is the first of three major creeks this route crosses. At Jonvick, the trail actually follows the crest of a massive beaver dam 150 yards around the edge of a scenic pond. The trail runs near the Lutsen Trail snowmobile trail for the next 3.5 miles, crossing it a few times and running on it for about half a mile.

After about crossing half a mile of dense, dark spruce forest, the trail climbs to the first of three classic North Shore "sawtooth" mountains. These ridgelines have a gradual slope down toward Lake Superior and a steep, even cliff-like, drop-off on the inland side. There are lovely views inland along these ridgelines, though you have to work for them a bit, sometimes stepping off the trail for a cliff-edge peak.

Spruce Creek cuts through the sawtooth ridge and provides a shaded lunch break spot on a smooth rock outcrop along the gurgling stream. The trail then climbs to the top of the second ridge, and you should keep looking for dramatic if somewhat hidden view points. The half-mile along a snowmobile trail might be a welcome break on a cloudy day or a hot slog in mid-August.

At the end of the second ridge there's the first big views of Lake Superior opening up ahead. You can see all the way to Grand Marais and even further up the North Shore. You can also take in the heart of Cascade River State Park laid out below you, including the full Cascade River valley. You're at over 1500 feet above sea level here, nine hundred feet higher than Lake Superior down below at the end of your hike.

The trail crosses Indian Camp Creek and passes the SHT campsite nearby.

After crossing Indian Camp Creek, there's a short climb to the final sawtooth ridgeline. This is Lookout Mountain, part of Cascade River State Park. Follow the Superior Hiking Trail signs and blue blazes through a series of trail junctions (onto a park ski trail, past a campsite and shelter) to the dramatic and popular Lookout Mountain overlook. This is your last big viewpoint of the day, so enjoy.

Keep following the SHT trail markers all the way down through Cascade State Park. Junctions and crossings get confusing, but the SHT markers will get you through. The last half mile goes down Cascade River, and you can pause at any of the scenic waterfalls that you see.

Hiking with your dog

Hiking with your canine companion can be great for the dog and great for you. But loose dogs can be bad for other hikers and local wildlife.

I like hiking with my dog…especially when she can run free off her leash. I love to watch her sprint and sniff through the woods. However, there are plenty of hikers out there who don't want your dog sniffing them or jumping on them. These hikers have the law on their side.

Here are the rules:

In **Minnesota state parks,** all pets must be on a leash six feet long or shorter. Dogs are allowed on the **Superior Hiking Trail** "on leash only." In the **Superior National Forest,** dogs can go off-leash on trails but must be on leash in developed recreational areas such as campgrounds.

Here's what I do:

Know your dog and the level of control you have. My dog would rather chase a pickup truck or bark at a passerby than come when I call. So she stays on the leash until I'm away from roads and reasonably sure that there are no other hikers around. If I want to let her run, I hike during mid-week or in off-seasons, and I choose trails that are out of the way. Check out the trails for "When you want to be alone" in "Andrew's picks" on page 8. I keep a lot of dog treats in my pockets, too.

When your dog does its business on the trail, please either bag it or at least kick it out into the woods.

38 Lookout Mountain

A *2.9 mile loop hike in Cascade River State Park near Lutsen*

State Park
Hiking
Club
TRAIL

Atop Lookout Mountain, you can see the vast and forested Cascade River valley.

▶ **What makes it unique.** Climb almost 500 feet to one of the North Shore's best state park high points.

▶ **Finding the trailhead.** At Highway 61 mile marker 100.0, enter Cascade River State Park. Follow park road into campground and park at trailhead parking lot.

▶ **State Park vehicle permit required.**

Lookout Mountain is a classic North Shore "sawtooth" mountain, like Moose Mountain (Hike # 35) and Leveaux Mountain (Hike #33). This hike includes much more than another viewpoint, however. It's a sampling of the best of Cascade River State Park: the river, the ridges, even the history.

This is a State Park Hiking Club Trail, so bring along your passport and watch for the password. Once you've finished, you'll surely agree with the password's description of the hike.

The hike is laid out like a figure eight on its side. You'll follow the Superior Hiking Trail for the top half of the fallen figure eight, and Cascade River State Park hiking trails for the bottom half. The loops intersect and cross at a foot-

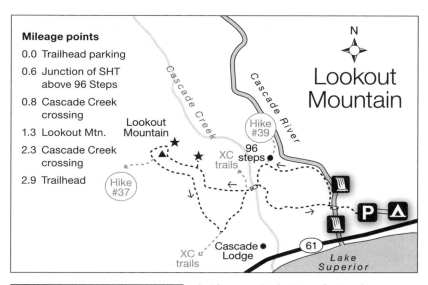

Mileage points

0.0 Trailhead parking

0.6 Junction of SHT above 96 Steps

0.8 Cascade Creek crossing

1.3 Lookout Mtn.

2.3 Cascade Creek crossing

2.9 Trailhead

N

Lookout Mountain

Lookout Mountain

Hike #39

96 steps

XC trails

Hike #37

XC trails

Cascade Lodge

61

Lake Superior

Distance: 2.9 miles

Time: 1.5 to 2.5 hours

Difficulty: moderate. It's a big climb to the top of Lookout Mountain. The trail is mostly wide and well-maintained.

More info:
Cascade River State Park
www.dnr.state.mn.us/state_
parks/cascade_river
(218) 387-6000
Map available online or at park office

GPS coordinates:
N47° 42.54'
W090° 31.28'

Trailhead facilities: Restrooms, vault toilet, campground, drinking water.

bridge over little Cascade Creek.

The start of the trail is clearly marked where it leads out of the state park campground. There are many intersections, but you can follow the signs for the Superior Hiking Trail, for the Hiking Club, and for the Lookout Mountain Trail: they all go to the same place.

Enjoy the scenic gorge of the Cascade River as you cross it and hike up above it for the first half mile. At a big, confusing intersection, do not go down the "96 steps"— that is the start of the seven-mile loop around the Cascade River. Instead, follow the other blue blazes as the Lookout Mountain trail curves away from the Cascade River and eventually crosses Cascade Creek.

The climb up the flank of Lookout Mountain is dramatic. What had recently been a thick and shady forest of birch and spruce trees has been transformed into open parkland by birch die-back and a big windstorm in September 2009.

A 2009 windstorm changed the upper loop dramatically (top); the forest is always changing, from ancient pine trees to today's dying birch trees (bottom).

After about one-quarter mile of climbing through this transformed forest, you'll reach a short spur to an overlook. There you'll find views to the north of a distant ridgeline and the Cascade River valley.

It's another quarter-mile to the final overlook on top of Lookout Mountain, a dramatic open area perched on the steep edge of the sawtooth. There's a big view looking east down to Lake Superior and the Cascade River valley snaking below. This is your scenic highlight for the day and well worth a long break. If you happen to need an outhouse, you'll find one at the campsite 80 yards farther along the trail.

Continue to follow the Hiking Club Trail signs past the campsite and shelter, briefly along a XC ski trail, then left onto a narrow hiking trail. You'll descend through a long stretch of dead and dying birch trees, eventually to connect with the Pioneer Trail, which is an old forest access road and a main XC ski trail

corridor in the winter. The Hiking Club Trail signs lead you along the Pioneer Trail for about 400 yards before you complete the Lookout Mountain Loop and recross Cascade Creek.

On the far side of Cascade Creek, the route turns right and follows state park trails back to the Cascade River.

▶ **Other options for this hike.** You can also start this hike from the mouth of the Cascade River on Highway 61 instead of driving into the park trailhead, following the trails up either side of the gorge to the large wooden footbridge.

Explore Cascade River State Park

Every North Shore river has waterfalls. But none of those rivers pack them in like the Cascade River. For its last half mile before meeting Lake Superior, the Cascade River drops nearly 200 feet, carving through a deep canyon.

But **Cascade River State Park** is much more than the river. It has the longest stretch of undeveloped Lake Superior shoreline. It has 18 miles of hiking and XC skiing trails. The river gorge is the most popular part of the park, leaving the lakeshore area and the trails to Lookout and Moose mountains for solitude and exploration.

Cascade River is the only North Shore state park with a private lodge right in the middle of it all. So you can stay at the park campground or in deluxe lodging and still be surrounded by the park. Tired and hungry at your campsite after your long hike around the Cascade River? Have dinner at **Cascade Lodge Restaurant and Pub**. Like a little luxury with your North Shore hiking experience? Hike out the door of your log cabin, and return to your own private whirlpool.

Whether you're at Cascade for a few hours or for a few days, be sure to visit the picnic area along the Lake Superior shoreline. You'll find easy access to the Lake's rugged shore and a lovely stand of old cedar and spruce trees.

39 Cascade River Loop

A 7.7 mile loop hike on the Superior Hiking Trail near Lutsen

Hidden Falls is a series of smaller falls along the upper Cascade River, accessible only by rugged hiking trails.

❱ **What makes it unique.** Hike deep into the rugged North Shore ridgeline on this long and challenging loop.

❱ **Finding the trailhead.** Park at the wayside at the mouth of the Cascade River, at mile marker 100, between Lutsen and Grand Marais.

The Cascade River is aptly named. Of all the North Shore rivers this one has the most dramatic final mile in its run to Lake Superior. It's one waterfall after another through a dark canyon. Above these falls, the river levels out a bit. This hike takes you on a grand tour of the river and its gorge as it cuts deep through the spine of the Sawtooth Mountains.

You could hike this loop in either direction, but this route travels clockwise up the west side. The start and end of the loop are on well-used state park trails, with viewing platforms that get you out to the best views on the waterfalls. The rest of the loop is challenging and often steep.

From the scenic and sturdy bridge about one-eighth mile up from the highway, you'll follow signs for the Superior Hiking Trail, both the blue blazes

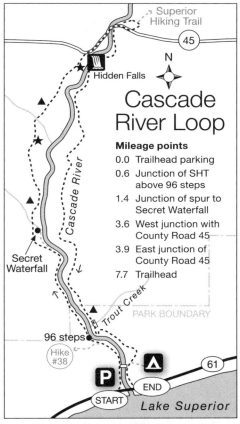

Cascade
River Loop

Mileage points

0.0 Trailhead parking
0.6 Junction of SHT above 96 steps
1.4 Junction of spur to Secret Waterfall
3.6 West junction with County Road 45
3.9 East junction of County Road 45
7.7 Trailhead

Distance: 7.7 miles

Time: 3 to 5 hours

Difficulty: difficult. Footing on the west side can be tricky and the climbs on both sides up and down the river valley are real challenges. You'll climb over 700 feet.

More info:
Superior Hiking Trail Assn.
www.superiorhiking.org
(218) 834-2700
Map Series E or McKenzie
Map 101: Cascade, Bally Creek

GPS coordinates:
N47° 42.42'
W090° 31.43'

Trailhead facilities: None. Restrooms, vault toilet, campground, drinking water, at park campground.

You'll descend the scenic 96 steps near the start of this hike.

and the Superior Hiking Trail logo signs. Be careful at a major intersection at mile 0.6. You'll take the Superior Hiking Trail down the "96 steps," a beautifully constructed set of steps and resting platforms.

The hike up the west side of the river involves climbing over many roots and rocks. At mile 1.4, a long spur trail leads to the Secret Waterfall. The trail climbs up and away from the river, and you won't see the Cascade River again for two miles. It's a great two miles of hiking with thigh-burning climbs and a gradual transition from pine trees and cedars on the riverbank to a maple forest on the

The trail on the west side of the Cascade River is full of roots and rocks.

ridge. The forest offers very pleasant hiking, with a smooth tread and, in the spring, a carpet of wildflowers.

Just before reaching County Road 45 (Pike Lake Road), check out the dramatic views of the Cascade's Hidden Falls area far below. Cross the Cascade on the county road bridge, loop back under the bridge on the northeast side, and continue down the east side of the river.

Massive white cedar trees crowd the edge of the river here as you approach Hidden Falls. Enjoy this wild and remote part of the trail; soon the trail becomes less interesting. The trail runs on private land for 1.5 miles, and after a steep uphill hike, the trail is a flat run along the top of the river valley edge, with decaying birch forest on the left and a noisy but invisible river down to the right.

Where private property ends, the trail descends through big pine trees to the river again and crosses Trout Creek. Note: the bridge over Trout Creek may be out; plan accordingly. Check current trail conditions at **www.superiorhiking. org/trail-conditions**. Follow the Superior Hiking Trail blazes carefully as the trail picks its way along XC ski trails and around a landslide restoration area.

Soon you're back on the park's wide, smooth walking trails around the lower falls and to the trailhead. Take a few minutes to visit the mouth of the Cascade River where it pours into Lake Superior.

▶ **Other options for this hike.** If 7.7 challenging miles is more than you want to take on, take the trail up the west side to the Secret Waterfall spur and return the way you came. This would be a total hike of about 3.5 miles.

Nearby **Eats, Treats & Lodging**

A pleasant campground can be found at Cascade River State Park—for more information see *Camping the North Shore,* by Andrew Slade. Grand Marais is just ten miles north, with lodging from campsites to condos and treats from tea to trout. Visit **www.visitcookcounty.com** for all the latest things to do and see.

40 Devil Track to Pincushion

A 7.2 mile out-and-back hike on the Superior Hiking Trail near Grand Marais

Andrew and Chloe head toward the bare rock summit of Pincushion Mountain.

▶ **What makes it unique.** Leading from the deep gorge of the Devil Track River to the dramatic bare rock summit of Pincushion Mountain, this hike takes you through unusual North Shore terrain.

▶ **Finding the trailhead.** About four miles east of Grand Marais on Highway 61, at mile marker 113.7, turn north on County Road 58 (Lindskog Road). Follow County Road 58 for 0.8 miles to Superior Hiking Trail parking lot on left.

Do you remember the story of the blind men and the elephant? Six blind men examine an elephant, each touching a different part. Asked what they are touching, the one by a leg says "a tree," one by the tail says "a broom," and one by the trunk says "a hose."

This fable has many different versions in other cultures. Think of it as you hike up the gorge of the Devil Track River. You will never quite see the gorge in its entirety, but you will experience parts of it from many perspectives. Put all the perspectives together and your will have your elephant...or your gorge.

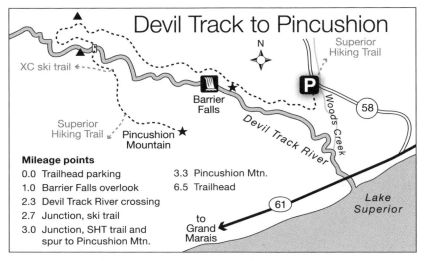

Devil Track to Pincushion

N
Superior Hiking Trail

XC ski trail

Barrier Falls

Superior Hiking Trail

Pincushion Mountain

Woods Creek

58

Devil Track River

61

Lake Superior

to Grand Marais

Mileage points

0.0 Trailhead parking	3.3 Pincushion Mtn.
1.0 Barrier Falls overlook	6.5 Trailhead
2.3 Devil Track River crossing	
2.7 Junction, ski trail	
3.0 Junction, SHT trail and spur to Pincushion Mtn.	

Distance: 6.5 miles

Time: 2.5 to 4 hours

Difficulty: moderate. Some steep climbs on decaying stairs or up bare rock make this well-marked trail a challenge.

More info:
Superior Hiking Trail Assn.
www.superiorhiking.org
(218) 834-2700
Map Series F or McKenzie Map 100: Grand Marais

GPS coordinates:
N47° 46.66'
W090° 15.93'

Trailhead facilities: None

The entire route is on the Superior Hiking Trail. Follow the Superior Hiking Trail blue or white blazes all the way.

At first you hike down Woods Creek rather than up the Devil Track River. Stick on the trail and you'll be to your first view of the Devil Track gorge in less than a quarter of a mile.

The hike goes up the east side of the Devil Track gorge for almost two miles, sometimes right on the edge.

There is no one great view into the gorge or down to waterfalls. Even at the landmark Barrier Falls Overlook, there's only a slight view past trees and cliffs of a distant waterfall. Here and there you'll see where other hikers have stepped off the trail toward the edge of the gorge for a better view. You can take all these little side paths, listen for the changing sound of the river below, and gather your own impressions.

The trail passes through a large stand of red pine trees. These appear to be from a fire, not from a plantation, since they are scattered and of different ages. The trail climbs a bit faster than the riverbed, so the gorge gets deeper and deeper as you go.

At the Barrier Falls overlook, you'll see the waterfall deep in the forested gorge below.

The most difficult part of the hike is crossing the gorge of the Devil Track River. In the course of a half mile, the trail descends 200 feet to the river, crosses the river on a remarkable A-frame bridge, and then climbs 150 feet up the other side. The Superior Hiking Trail register is on the west bank of the bridge for you to record your thoughts.

Once you've reached the other side of the gorge, take a rest on the big bench, then complete the journey to Pincushion Mountain. Signs guide you across a wide trail, part of the Pincushion Mountain XC ski system, and you will cross these XC trails twice. In a half mile, there's a sign for the spur trail to Pincushion Mountain overlook.

Now you're following white blazes, the Superior Hiking Trail's official spur trail marking. It's just a hundred yards through the woods, and then you're up on top of Pincushion Mountain itself.

Pincushion Mountain is unique on the North Shore. It is nearly bare rock for 300 yards, with dramatic views of the shoreline and Lake Superior. Grasses and lichens and spindly trees stick out of the rock, giving it the look of an actual pincushion. Follow the white blazes all the way to the end of the mountaintop, where you'll find a vista that spreads from the Grand Marais harbor on the right to the distant Lake Superior shoreline to the left, and far across Lake Superior.

From the top, see if you can find the Devil Track gorge off to the north. For such a distinctive feature, it's hard to pick out from above.

After lunch and sightseeing, pack up and head back the way you came.

⏵ **Other options for this hike.** Do a one-way shuttle hike: you'll hike to the Grand Marais Overlook off the Gunflint Trail. From the base of Pincushion Mountain, continue on the Superior Hiking Trail route, all the way to the Grand Marais Overlook. This is a shorter hike, just 4.5 miles. Contact Harriet Quarles Transportation for shuttle service, 866-387-1801 or harrietq@boreal.org.

Explore Artist's Point and Sweethearts Bluff

Grand Marais is surrounded by wild places. Vast Lake Superior and the expansive Boundary Waters are short drives or paddles from the harbor town. Wild lands are also right in town. From downtown Grand Marais, you can walk out and explore the scenic nooks and crannies of Artist's Point or the rugged terrain of Sweethearts Bluff.

Found to the east and south of downtown Grand Marais, **Artist's Point** (pictured above) combines a conifer-clad island, open shelves of bedrock, and the harbor break wall. You can walk along the rocks and break wall all the way to the lighthouse, or head the opposite direction along ledge rock to a great view of open Lake Superior and the distant shoreline.

Walk through the Grand Marais RV Park and Campground to **Sweethearts Bluff**, where you'll find a network of trails ranging from a short wheelchair-accessible loop to a mile-plus journey to the site of a former lookout tower.

41 Eagle Mountain

A 7.2 mile out-and-back hike in the Boundary Waters Canoe Area north of Lutsen

From the top of Eagle Mountain, the view stretches out for miles, including BWCA lakes and distant North Shore ridges.

▶ **What makes it unique.** Climb to the highest point in Minnesota and at least for a moment, stand alone on top of the state.

▶ **Finding the trailhead.** From Highway 61 mile marker 92.0, take County Road 4 (Caribou Trail) 17.5 miles to its end at a T-junction with Forest Road 170 (The Grade). Turn right and go 3.8 miles to marked trailhead parking on left. If you're coming from the Grand Marais area, you can drive up past Devil Track Lake on county roads 8 and 158—ask locally for directions.

▶ **BWCA day permit required;** available at trailhead.

This is a hike for the patriotic. If you love Minnesota, you owe it to yourself to get to the top of Eagle Mountain, which is the highest point in the state.

It's a case of the end justifying the means. The hike into the base of Eagle Mountain is rather flat and monotonous over rough terrain. The hike up the ridge to the top is dramatic and a good physical challenge.

Fill out your day permit at the trailhead sign, put one copy in the box and bring the other with you. Since this hike enters the BWCA Wilderness, you must follow wilderness rules about group size (9 people maximum), containers (no metal or glass), and motors (no dirt bikes).

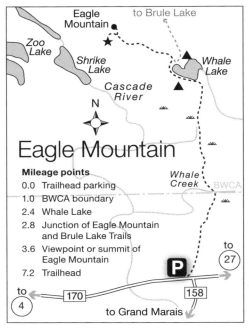

Eagle Mountain to Brule Lake

Zoo Lake

Shrike Lake

Whale Lake

Cascade River

N

Eagle Mountain

Mileage points
0.0 Trailhead parking
1.0 BWCA boundary
2.4 Whale Lake
2.8 Junction of Eagle Mountain and Brule Lake Trails
3.6 Viewpoint or summit of Eagle Mountain
7.2 Trailhead

Whale Creek BWCA

P

to 27

to 4

170

158

to Grand Marais

Distance: 7.2 miles

Time: 2.5 to 4 hours

Difficulty: difficult. The approach hike covers rocky, rough terrain, and the hike to the summit is steep, climbing 400 feet in a half mile.

More info:
Superior National Forest
Gunflint Ranger District
(218) 387-1750
Voyageur Map 9: Gunflint Lake or McKenzie Map 3: Ball Club, Winchell and Poplar lakes

GPS coordinates:
N47° 51.80'
W090° 32.75'

Trailhead facilities: Vault toilet, picnic table.

The trail starts wide, thanks to trail improvements dedicated to Robbie Tyler of St. Louis Park, Minnesota, who died in Mali on a 1992 adventure. The forest is made up of boreal tree species such as jackpine, spruce and fir.

It's over two miles from the trailhead on a rocky trail to scenic Whale Lake. You can keep track of your progress by counting the boardwalks: there are three sets of boardwalks total. You cross the first set right after entering the BWCA, about halfway to Whale Lake. The second boardwalk is three-quarters of the way to Whale Lake, and goes through a bog forest of tamarack and leatherleaf. The third boardwalk is close

Whale Lake sits at the base of Eagle Mountain and its unnamed sister peak, shown here.

to Whale Lake. There's a very short unmarked spur after the third boardwalk to an open view of a beaver pond; this is the first open view in almost two miles.

Finally you reach the south shore of Whale Lake, with a gorgeous view.

Across the lake, a dramatic hill rises from the forest. This is not Eagle Mountain, but instead an unnamed peak just 100 feet shorter and to its east.

The trail follows the shore of Whale Lake for one-third of a mile, passing a rough BWCA campsite in the woods and a number of scenic sitting areas.

Before beginning the climb to the top of Eagle Mountain, consider taking a lakeshore lunch break. From the junction of the Eagle Mountain and Brule Lake trails, take the Brule Lake trail about 100 yards to a junction. Here, the Brule Lake trail goes left and a rougher trail goes straight ahead. You can follow this rough trail about 80 yards to a lakeshore BWCA campsite, complete with benches around a fireplace and a wilderness latrine.

The climb to the summit starts near the junction of the Eagle Mountain trail and the Brule Lake trail. It's a steep climb right at the start, scampering up exposed bedrock through spruce trees and birch trees. You can see that you're climbing a ridge as the terrain visibly drops off to the left.

Eventually, you get the first dramatic view, due south over the watershed of the Cascade River toward hidden Lake Superior. You're at about 2,260 feet here; the trail continues farther along another 400 yards or so to the big views of the summit.

There are two very different places to go on top of Eagle Mountain: the big view and the big high point. The big view of the surrounding terrain is very easy to find. A wide-open area of red granite bedrock

The Brule Lake trail begins its long route west near the base of Eagle Mountain.

has scattered jackpine trees that frame the views. You're looking southwest out over the BWCA, across seldom-paddled lakes Shrike, Zoo and Eagle. Far in the distance you can pick out Lichen Lake and Cascade Lake.

The big high point is a little harder to find. Follow rock cairns inland from the viewpoint until you reach a small clearing in the woods with a plaque and smaller survey markers. There is no view from here, just good feelings as you stand on top of Minnesota.

Nearby Eats, Treats & Lodging

Eagle Mountain is in a very remote part of the Superior National Forest. Pleasant camping near the trailhead can be found at Crescent Lake and Devil Track Lake campgrounds. Both are featured in *Camping the North Shore,* by Andrew Slade.

Read the history of the measurement of Minnesota's highest peak on the plaque. There is a significant error here: Ulysses Sherman Grant, who accompanied state geologist Newton Winchell in the 1890s measuring these peaks, is not in fact "the president's son," but an unrelated geology student at the University of Minnesota. Another historical debate is obvious here:

Rock cairns lead inland to a plaque marking the summit of Eagle Mountain.

the Arrowhead Chapter of Minnesota Society of Professional Surveyors put a survey mark here in 2002 that says the elevation is 2,298.15 feet, not the 2,301 feet measured in 1961. Either way, it's Minnesota's highest point.

Take your time at the top of Eagle Mountain, then begin the steep descent and the long walk back.

❱ **Other options for this hike.** With an overnight BWCA reservation, this could be a weekend backpacking trip. Hike in to Whale Lake in the afternoon, set up camp by the lakeshore, then climb the mountain at first light the next day.

Who are the "Highpointers?"

Who is that dude dashing down from the top of Eagle Mountain? He's from Iowa, he slept in the back of his truck last night, and tomorrow he'll be somewhere in Wisconsin. He is a Highpointer, trying to reach the high point of all 50 states.

Highpointers have their own club, their own website **(highpointers.org)**, their own logo and more.

Eagle Mountain surprises many of these Highpointers as they sweep through the Midwest. The trail is more rugged and steep than any other in the region. As one blogger wrote on www.americasroof.com, "Highpointers expecting another Midwestern corn field or grassy knoll for a high point are in for a big surprise."

As a result of being Minnesota's high point, the Eagle Mountain trail is one of the most used in the Superior National Forest. Expect to have company on the trail and at the summit almost any day in summer or fall. Take a moment to chat with your fellow hikers; they often have great stories to tell.

42 Caribou Rock Trail

An 8.0 mile out-and-back hike in the Superior National Forest off the Gunflint Trail

photo: © Bryan Hansel, www.bryanhansel.com

Look out across Rose Lake to Canada at the end of this dramatic hike.

▶ **What makes it unique.** This is one of the most challenging hikes in the North Shore area and has the most beautiful inland lake views.

▶ **Finding the trailhead.** From Grand Marais, follow County Road 12 (Gunflint Trail) 30 miles to County Road 21 (Hungry Jack Road). Drive 1.9 miles on County Road 21, past Leo Lake, to trailhead parking on right side of road.

▶ **BWCA day permit required;** at trailhead.

With great challenges come great rewards. Plan on taking a full day for this hike, and pack a hearty lunch to enjoy at Rose Lake. After the scenic first three-quarters mile, the trail gets difficult, with steep climbs and even steeper descents, through rough, beautiful forest.

It's highly recommended to bring a map and compass on this hike to monitor your progress and to identify the lakes. The thick forest and cliffs block the satellite access your GPS unit requires.

Fill out your BWCA day permit at the trailhead. Wilderness rules limit your group to nine people; no glass bottles or metal cans are allowed.

About halfway through the hike, the trail crosses the broad and open portage

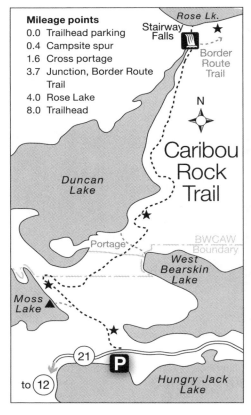

Mileage points
0.0 Trailhead parking
0.4 Campsite spur
1.6 Cross portage
3.7 Junction, Border Route Trail
4.0 Rose Lake
8.0 Trailhead

Distance: 8.0 miles

Time: 6 to 8 hours

Difficulty: difficult. This wilderness trail is roughly built and has steep climbs and descents.

More info:
Superior National Forest
(218) 387-1750
Voyageur Map 9: Gunflint Lake or McKenzie Map 2: E. Bearskin Lake or Fisher Map F-13: North Gunflint Trail

GPS coordinates:
N48° 03.66'
W090° 27.36'

Trailhead facilities: None

between West Bearskin Lake and Duncan Lake. Plan to check your timing and your energy levels here to see if you can continue the hike all the way to Rose Lake and back.

The trail weaves among four beautiful lakes. The views start right away, with a great overlook of West Bearskin after a brief climb from the parking lot. This is the actual Caribou Rock. This first section of trail is wide and well-maintained, running along a ridgeline. After the trail passes great views of West Bearskin, it pops out for a view of Moss Lake.

Watch for a spur trail to a campsite; the trail takes a sharp right turn at the spur junction. Soon after, you'll cross into the BWCA Wilderness and hit one last big view of Moss Lake.

Heading north from Moss Lake, the trail gets rougher and steeper. There are four humps of about 200 feet to climb up and down...each way. On the way north, the climbs up are on rocky slopes with big pine trees. The descents are down steep clefts of dark cedar forest. Reverse this for the return trip.

Keep an eye on the trail at all times. With all the boulders and the big downed trees and the rough trail construction, it is easy to get off the trail. Stop and check your progress when you reach the big wide portage. The portage comes right after crossing a very rocky creek bed. The trail does not get any easier after this halfway spot.

Duncan Lake is in view for much of the hike.

The final descent takes you down to the northern tip of Duncan Lake and to Rose Lake and the Stairway Portage connecting Duncan and Rose. The Caribou Rock Trail meets the main Border Route Trail.

Take a left here to explore Stairway Portage, Stairway Falls, and the shores of Rose Lake. Then, should time permit, hike east on the Border Route Trail up to the Rose Cliffs for the best lake view of the day, out across Rose Lake to the Canadian wilderness beyond.

After you've seen the sights, you may want to take a swim to cool off on a hot day before you begin the long and strenuous trip back to the trailhead.

▶ **Other options for this hike.** With prior planning, you could do an unusual shuttle by canoe on this trail. Half your party could paddle canoes in from West Bearskin Lake and the other half could hike the trail. Then you could meet at the Stairway Portage and switch for the ride back. Each party should have its own BWCA day permit.

Nearby *Eats,* Treats & Lodging

Hungry Jack Lodge is a full-service resort located right near the trailhead. After a fire in 2008, the main lodge was rebuilt and includes a restaurant for tired hikers. Back at the Gunflint Trail is Trail Center Lodge, a restaurant and bar on Poplar Lake. Campers can stay at Hungry Jack Lodge's campground or at the Superior National Forest campgrounds on East Bearskin or Flour Lakes.

Big pine trees stand near the shore of Duncan Lake.

43 Bryce Breon Trail

A 5.2 mile loop on the Border Route Trail off the Gunflint Trail

From the South Rim Trail, hikers find great views of Gunflint Lake.

▶ **What makes it unique.** In a land torn apart by fire and windstorms, here is a magical stretch of intact forest, as well as great views of Gunflint Lake.

▶ **Finding the trailhead.** From Grand Marais, take County Road 12 (Gunflint Trail) 41 miles to the Loon Lake public landing. Park at parking area above boat landing area.

Explore this wonderful Gunflint Trail stretch of old-growth cedar and dramatic views of Gunflint Lake. The loop combines the Bryce Breon Trail with parts of the Border Route Trail and the Upper Gunflint XC ski trails.

The first 2.5 miles up to the overlook are on the Bryce Breon Trail, named after two late members of the Minnesota Rovers. This trail was built to be a wilderness XC ski trail. The trail parallels the north shore of Loon Lake through huge cedar trees for almost two miles. There is one scenic lake access point, on a shelf of rock that could make for great swimming.

The Bryce Breon Trail is in deep woods where the shade prevents grass from growing. That can make it good hiking through the summer. In the spring, you may find yourself crossing inlets of the lake and jumping from one huge cedar root to another. The last part of the Bryce Breon Trail climbs away from

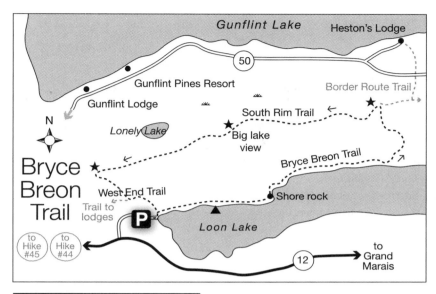

Bryce
Breon
Trail

Distance: 5.2 miles

Time: 2 to 3 hours

Difficulty: moderate. The wide trail has tricky footing in places.

More info:
Border Route Trail Association
www.borderroutetrail.org
McKenzie Map 4: Gunflint Lake or
Voyageur Map 9: Gunflint Lake

GPS coordinates:
N48° 04.44'
W090° 44.23'

Trailhead facilities: Vault toilet

Mileage points

0.0 Trailhead parking

0.8 Shore rock

2.5 Junction of Bryce Breon and South Rim Trails

3.7 Big lake view

4.9 Junction of South Rim and West End Trails

5.2 Trailhead

Loon Lake through a magical grove of cedars. In the spring, a rivulet runs right through the cedar trees, cascading over their roots.

At the junction with the South Rim Trail, take a long break to enjoy the view down toward Gunflint Lake. This is one of the two best views along this route, so take your time.

The route follows the South Rim Trail west for two miles. There are many dead trees still on the ground from the famous 1999 blowdown and most of the forest is young and recovering, though the 12-foot aspen, dogwood and alder trees block your views. The best viewpoints are a little over a mile along the South Rim Trail and the rest is like walking through a tunnel. You might find a grassy trail in summer. The last half mile of the route takes you over the top of a barren ridgeline to a junction with the West End XC ski trail. Turn right here if you wish to reach Gunflint Lodge. Turn left on the West End trail to return to

The Loon Lake shoreline invites hikers to rest and swim.

the Loon Lake boat landing and complete the loop.

▶ **Other options for this hike.** This loop connects to the lodges on Gunflint Lake, so you could access the trail directly from them.

Nearby **Eats, Treats & Lodging**

Gunflint Lodge has two dining options to start or end your day of hiking. Next door, Gunflint Pines Resort serves pizza and burgers. Heston's Lodge has been a long-time supporter of the Border Route Trail. All are good options for an overnight stay.

Mountain lions: the ultimate solo hiker

Lions and tigers and bears? On the North Shore, you've got them all…if you count the Canada lynx as the tiger. Sightings of mountain lions in the North Shore area are rare but

photo: istockphoto.com

seem to be on the increase. Should you be worried about lions, like Dorothy was in the Wizard of Oz?

In a word, no. While sightings are rare, there have been zero incidents of mountain lions injuring people in Minnesota.

Instead of worrying about mountain lions, try to admire them. Mountain lions are the ultimate solo adventurer, living mostly alone and seldom sticking around to defend a home territory. Instead they walk for hundreds of miles, over a range of nearly 300 square miles. If you see one as you're hiking the North Shore, consider yourself very lucky…and safe.

44 Magnetic Rock Trail

A 3.2 mile out-and-back hike in the Superior National Forest off the Gunflint Trail

The landmark Magnetic Rock looms over a burned down forest.

❯ What makes it unique. A journey through terrain both blown down and burned away culminates in a visit to a lonely landmark, mysterious Magnetic Rock.

❯ Finding the trailhead. From Grand Marais, follow County Road 12 (Gunflint Trail) 48 miles to trailhead parking on the right. This is just a few hundred yards past the Kekekabic Trail trailhead (Hike #45) on the left.

Catastrophic forces have been at work here, with a massive blowdown in 1999, a prescribed burn in 2002, and big forest fires in 2006 (Cavity Lake) and 2007 (Ham Lake). What had been an interesting walk through the woods is now a journey across a barren landscape. And what had been a hard-to-see mystery rock is now a towering landmark visible through dead trees nearly a quarter mile away.

Because so much of this trail runs across solid rock or very thin soil, the vegetation here will take longer to return than other Gunflint trails such as the nearby Centennial Trail (Hike #45). Unless another big fire rolls through, the vegetation will have filled in enough so that these dramatic open views will be gone within a decade.

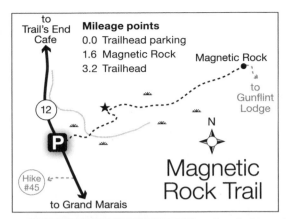

Mileage points
0.0 Trailhead parking
1.6 Magnetic Rock
3.2 Trailhead

to Trail's End Cafe

Magnetic Rock

to Gunflint Lodge

N

to Grand Marais

Magnetic Rock Trail

Distance: 3.2 miles

Time: 1 to 2 hours

Difficulty: moderate. The terrain is flat and open, though a lack of cairns or blazes in the open area might challenge your route finding.

More info:
Superior National Forest
(218) 387-1750
Voyageur Map 6: Saganaga Lake or McKenzie Map 7: Tuscarora

GPS coordinates:
N48° 05.51'
W090° 49.52'

Trailhead facilities: Latrine, picnic table.

A cairn made of dark-colored iron formation and light-colored tonalite is found along the trail.

Magnetic Rock is the destination of this hike, but the journey itself is fascinating. Much of the route is on bare and open rock, the same type of rock that Magnetic Rock itself is made of. In fact, the bedrock underfoot along the way has the same compass-altering powers as the towering Magnetic Rock. The rock is a banded iron formation, and it shows off all sorts of layers and colors.

The first quarter mile of the trail is in forest that survived the blowdown and the fires. Right away you'll see the massive sloping slabs of magnetic bedrock on the edge of a little marsh. After crossing a little creek in a crack, the trail leaves the forest and heads into open terrain, making a big swooping climb up to an open ridgeline. From this ridgeline, you can see 360 degrees through a blown-down, burned-down landscape.

This is a geologist's dream setting. Watch for two very different kinds of rock along this trail. The bedrock has a banded iron formation, rich in minerals such as magnetite. You'll also see this in the dark, angular chunks that make up cairns. If you brought a compass, pass it closely by any of these dark rocks and watch the needle swing. With a good eye you can even pick out stromatolites, fossils of blue-green algae from nearly two billion years ago.

The second kind of rock you'll see is a very light-colored, often rounded rock with darker speckles. This is tonalite, a granitic

Andrew stands at the base of Magnetic Rock (top); pass a compass over the exposed iron rocks and watch the needle spin (bottom).

rock found in large formations just north of this trail and carried here by glaciers.

After cresting over a second gentle ridge and picking your way around young jackpine trees, you'll see the star of the hike, the Magnetic Rock itself.

Magnetic Rock appears to be about 25 feet high. Look around behind the rock and you'll see what looks like a quarry; it seems that the big rock could have been ripped out of the surrounding bedrock and simply tipped on its edge. Was it ancient humans with Stonehenge-like technology who lifted it up? Or was it a massive glacier? Groovy markings in the banded iron formation add to the mystery. Is that a Thunderbird symbol, or just veins of minerals?

When you've fully explored the mysteries of Magnetic Rock, return the way you came.

▶ Other options for this hike. This trail is the western terminus of the Border Route Trail, the rugged 65-mile long hiking trail that runs all the way to the Arrowhead Trail near Grand Portage. For a day hike with a vehicle shuttle, you can continue on this trail about four miles to Gunflint Lodge.

If you have a full day, you can combine this hike with the Centennial Trail (Hike #45) for two very different hikes totaling almost 7 miles.

Nearby **Eats, Treats & Lodging**

There are many lodges located on Gunflint Lake, with full services. Nearby, at the very end of the Gunflint Trail, is the remote Trail's End Café. Plus, camping is terrific at the Trail's End Campground, featured in *Camping the North Shore*, by Andrew Slade. More info on lodging and amenities can be found at **www.visitcookcounty.com**.

45 Centennial Trail

A 3.4 mile loop hike in the Superior National Forest off the Gunflint Trail

Across the burned and blown-down landscape, Loon Lake is just visible in the far distance.

❱ **What makes it unique.** Hike through the heart of the 2007 Ham Lake Fire and watch forest history unfold. Interpretive signs add meaning to the experience.

❱ **Finding the trailhead.** Take County Road 12 (Gunflint Trail) 47 miles from Grand Marais to parking lot on left.

This is one of the most unusual hikes you can take in northeastern Minnesota, due to recent forest fires and the 1999 blowdown. There is little shade along this route, so plan accordingly on sunny days.

The Centennial Trail links together trails with histories dating back to the 1800s. The first part, going west, is on the Kekekabic Trail; this part of "The Kek" was built in the 1880s to access iron mining operations on Miner Lake. The second part of the route follows the bed of a mining railroad line built in 1892. The trail was opened in 2009 as part of the celebration of the Superior National Forest centennial celebration.

Pick up a copy of the interpretive brochure or download it from the Superior National Forest website; search for "centennial trail gunflint."

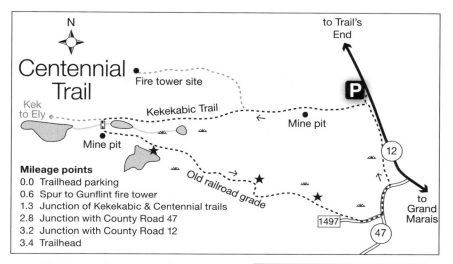

Centennial Trail

Mileage points
0.0 Trailhead parking
0.6 Spur to Gunflint fire tower
1.3 Junction of Kekekabic & Centennial trails
2.8 Junction with County Road 47
3.2 Junction with County Road 12
3.4 Trailhead

The blown-down trees from the 1999 straight-line winds all point the same direction: east-northeast. The 2007 Ham Lake Fire burned over the whole area but wasn't hot or slow enough to burn through the logs themselves, so the bulk of the logs remain. To learn more about this landscape, read *Gunflint Burning: Fire in the Boundary Waters,* by Cary J. Griffith.

The route goes almost straight west, due to a natural crease in the earth that is made much more visible by the lack of standing trees. It's a geologic fault line, in which a series of creek beds have developed over the centuries since the glaciers retreated. Beavers have been busy along the line, creating and maintaining a series of ponds. You'll be walking downstream, though the loss of elevation isn't noticeable.

The area's mining history is very evident. The trail goes by two large test pits from 1893, both now full of water.

After 1.3 miles, the Centennial Trail breaks off of the Kekekabic Trail and crosses the creek before turning back east. The trail climbs up ridges, where good views open up of the surrounding ponds and distant hills. At the first

Distance: 3.4 miles

Time: 1.5 to 2.5 hours

Difficulty: difficult. Rough trail conditions and lack of shade make it challenging, especially in mid-summer.

More info:
Superior National Forest
(218) 387-1750
Map available from Superior National Forest

GPS coordinates:
N48° 05.36'
W090° 49.43'

Trailhead facilities: None

A few miles farther on the Kekekabic Trail, Bingshik Lake has a small campsite.

ridge top, look across the lake to the far shore; this was the site of Gunflint City in the 1890s.

The trail becomes suspiciously overbuilt, your clue that you're following an old railroad bed. The Port Arthur, Duluth and Western Railway was built to connect the Paulson Mine with Port Arthur (today's Thunder Bay, Ontario), 91 track miles away and 1,200 feet down in elevation. It was a seven-hour journey, open to passengers as far as Gunflint Lake. Apparently only one load of ore went out on these tracks. The trail had been largely forgotten until the fires of 2006 and 2007 opened up the forest. There's a steep climb to a great view six miles out to Loon Lake.

The last half mile of the trail uses a series of roads and snowmobile trails before finally reaching County Road 12 (Gunflint Trail) and the trailhead. In the days of mining, this area was the site of a huge switchback up the steep railroad grade. Follow the signs carefully to make sure you stay on track.

▶ **Other options for this hike.** At a half mile in, a spur trail leads up to a high point of 2064 feet, the former site of the Gunflint fire tower. The tower was last used in 1956 and torn down in 1979.

From the junction where the Centennial Trail goes to the south, you can continue 2.2 miles straight ahead on the Kekekabic Trail past Mine Lake to Bingshik Lake. At Bingshik Lake, head for the first campsite right on the lake. It's an official BWCA campsite complete with fire grate and latrine.

If you're planning to go all the way to Bingshik Lake, register for a BWCA wilderness day permit at the trailhead.

The Kekekabic Trail

Decades before the Superior Hiking Trail, another long-distance trail called adventurous hikers for dramatic backcountry adventures. The **Kekekabic Trail** was originally built to provide access to a ranger cabin and fire tower on Kekekabic Lake, deep in the Superior National Forest. It runs 40 miles from Snowbank Lake, outside of Ely, to the Gunflint Trail near Gunflint Lake. Strategically placed campsites make it possible to spend a few days or a week hiking the route.

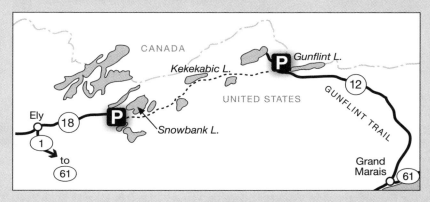

"The Kek" is a true wilderness trail, since most of it is within the BWCA. Maintenance is only done with hand tools and there is no real trail blazing or signage. Only experienced hikers with very good navigation skills should backpack on the trail. Even on short day hikes such as the Centennial Trail (Hike #45), caution is advised. The 1999 blowdown and subsequent forest fires nearly erased the trail, but dedicated volunteers and the Superior National Forest repaired the damage. For more information, visit **www.northcountrytrail.org/trail/minnesota/kek**.

46 Devil's Kettle

A 2.0 mile out-and-back hike in Magney State Park near Hovland

The Brule River carves through its deep canyon in Judge C.R. Magney State Park. Upper Falls is visible on the right.

▶ **What makes it unique.** The Devil's Kettle is a real North Shore mystery, and the hike to get there is the perfect blend of accessibility and challenge.

▶ **Finding the trailhead.** From Grand Marais, Judge C.R. Magney State Park is 24 miles east on Highway 61, at mile marker 124.0. Drive past the contact station and past the turnoff for the campground to the large trailhead parking area at the end of the road. The trail starts from the parking lot.

▶ **State Park vehicle permit required.**

This is a wide and easy trail along a classic North Shore river valley to a local landmark, the Devil's Kettle, where the Brule River splits into two; one half of the river disappears into a cauldron.

The Devil's Kettle Trail is the park's official Hiking Club Trail, so you can bring along your Hiking Club Trail passbook and watch for the password.

If you're staying at the campground, you'll find the trail right at the base of the campground road.

Pick up the trail where the footbridge crosses the Brule River from the camp-

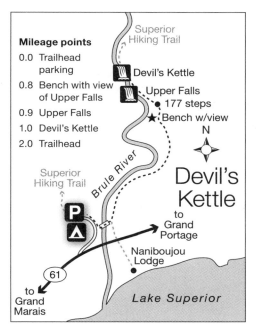

Superior Hiking Trail

Devil's Kettle
Upper Falls
● 177 steps
★ Bench w/view
N

Superior Hiking Trail
Brule River

Devil's Kettle
to Grand Portage
Naniboujou Lodge
●
61
to Grand Marais
Lake Superior

Distance: 2.0 miles

Time: 1 to 1.5 hours

Difficulty: easy. Although there are nearly 200 steps to descend and climb, the trail is wide and easy.

More info:
Judge C.R. Magney State Park
(218) 387-6300
www.dnr.state.mn.us/state_parks/judge_cr_magney/

GPS coordinates:
N47° 49.14'
W090° 03.11'

Trailhead facilities: Vault toilet, campground, drinking water, picnic area.

ground and parking lot. Stop for a moment at the plaque dedicating the park to Judge Clarence Reinhold Magney, a mayor of Duluth and a Minnesota Supreme Court Justice who many consider to be the father of North Shore state parks.

The wide trail runs along the east bank of the Brule River, gradually climbing to higher overlooks through birch and fir forests.

There's a great little turn-off at about the three-quarter mile mark, with a pleasant bench and a view into the river valley to Upper Falls. You may ask yourself, if this is Upper Falls, where is Lower Falls? Eve and Gary Wallinga, in their fine book *Waterfalls of the North Shore,* claim that you can follow a steep narrow trail from this overlook about 0.2 miles down to the river to see the 7-foot drop of Lower Falls.

The biggest challenge of the Devil's Kettle hike is the many steps. Some have counted 177 steps...see what count you get. The steps are well built, with sturdy handrails and platforms with benches to rest on.

As you descend the steps, your senses come alive with the sights, sounds and smells of a rushing North Shore river valley.

Once you reach the river edge, the first landmark is a very short spur to the base of Upper Falls. In spring run-off, you can hang out on a rock ledge above the torrent and get damp from the mist.

Return to the trail and hike another 150 yards to Devil's Kettle. Two viewing platforms hang over the river gorge for different views of the famous mystery falls. Check both viewpoints, and then head another few yards up the trail for an intimate riverside rest stop.

When you've had your fill of this unusual and scenic area, return the way you came...*up* all those steps.

▶ **Other options for this hike.** The Superior Hiking Trail continues past Devil's Kettle, but turns much narrower and more difficult. You can continue hiking another 3.8 miles to County Road 70 (Camp 20 Road).

Explore Judge C.R. Magney State Park

Acre for acre, Judge C.R. Magney State Park is the least developed of the North Shore state parks. The trail system penetrates only a small portion of the park. The park has a pleasant open campground, which was built on the site of the 1934 Works Progress Administration camp. This campground is a great base for exploring the tip of the Arrowhead area, perfect for day trips to the Grand Portage area and the Arrowhead Trail.

Near the campground, two trails head off into the park. One is a four-mile loop to a shelter and overlooks of the Brule River. The other is a self-guided nature outing known as the Timberdoodle Trail.

One highlight of the park experience isn't actually in the park. Head across Highway 61 to the Naniboujou Lodge, where you can dine in the restaurant with its amazing painted walls. After your delicious meal, enjoy the cobblestone Lake Superior beach.

47 Border Route Trail Sampler

A 5.2 mile out-and-back hike on the Border Route Trail, near Hovland

South Fowl Lake unfolds below the Border Route Trail and the Pigeon River cliffs.

▶ **What makes it unique.** Try this short, easy-to-reach eastern section sampler of the rugged and remote Border Route Trail.

▶ **Finding the trailhead.** From the town of Hovland, turn north on County Road 16 (Arrowhead Trail). Drive 18.3 miles on this increasingly scenic road past McFarland Lake to the Border Route Trail parking lot on the right side of the road.

There are two really good reasons to drive all this way for this hike. First, it gets you into beautiful country you may have never seen before. Before you even leave your car, you'll see the dramatic terrain of the McFarland Lake area. High ridges rise right out of scenic lakes, and the views from the top of those ridges stretch into Canada. The border lakes area in the tip of the Arrowhead has a geologic story unique to Minnesota, the result of which are long narrow lakes edged by steep cliffs.

The second reason is to experience the Border Route Trail.

This round trip hike gives you a taste of the Border Route Trail's level of difficulty, without committing you to a major wilderness expedition. It climbs gradually but insistently to the top of a ridge, with beautiful glimpses of the lakes and rivers below.

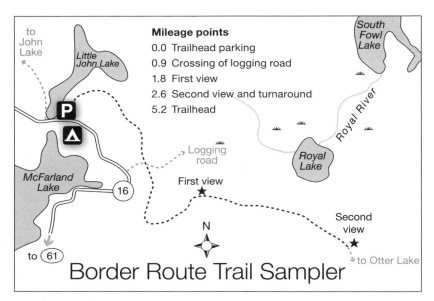

Mileage points
0.0 Trailhead parking
0.9 Crossing of logging road
1.8 First view
2.6 Second view and turnaround
5.2 Trailhead

Border Route Trail Sampler

Distance: 5.2 miles

Time: 2 to 3 hours

Difficulty: difficult. Like most of the Border Route Trail, this section is tricky underfoot and may be hard to follow, especially in late summer.

More info:
Border Route Trail Association
www.borderroutetrail.org
McKenzie Map 1: Pine Lake
or Voyageur Map 10: East
Bearskin Lake

GPS coordinates:
N48° 03.25'
W090° 03.35'

Trailhead facilities: vault toilet, campground.

The Border Route Trail can be hard to follow; the tread is not well-established and the trail may not be recently brushed. The main signage is blue flagging tied to trees and branches. This section appears to get some of the best maintenance.

Starting from the parking lot, you'll find the Border Route Trail headed off to the east, marked by a simple wooden sign. For the first third of a mile, the trail winds through old aspen forest. Keep an eye out for the blue flagging. After the aspen forest, the trail winds through a long stretch of pleasant and shady cedar swamp and forest. The only landmark is an old logging road that the trail crosses.

After nearly 1.5 miles of gradual ascent, the trail turns sharply to the east-northeast and begins a serious climb. This is open terrain, logged in the last decade. Hiking here can be hot in summer as there is no shade in the steepest part of the climb. Tall grass may grow over the trail during the summer, since there's so much more sunshine compared to the deep forest.

The trail levels off right before the first viewpoint, where there's a narrow opening to the north-northeast. There's a view there of the Royal River and distant South Fowl Lake. The trail continues along the edge of the high ridge, with scattered partial views through cedar and white pine to the terrain 300 feet below. It's almost a mile to the next viewpoint and the turnaround spot. This is a more dramatic view, taking in South Fowl Lake and the Pigeon River cliffs.

Find a shady, breezy spot here for lunch, then return the way you came.

Nearby **Eats, Treats & Lodging**

There are no services up the Arrowhead Trail, not even a resort selling an overpriced can of cold pop. You will find a small, free campground right across the road from the trailhead for this hike. It's managed by the Minnesota Department of Natural Resources along with the McFarland Lake boat landing.

The Border Route Trail

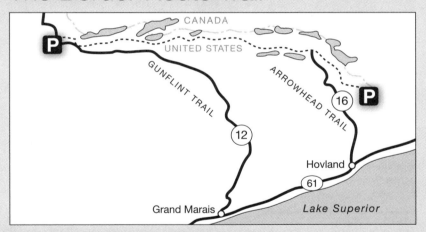

Is the Superior Hiking Trail too cushy for you? Are there too many bridges over streams? Too many handrails on those steps? Just can't stand seeing other *people* every 20 minutes? If you're accustomed to the Superior Hiking Trail, you'll find the **Border Route Trail** less maintained and less accessible. You'll also find it equal to the SHT in scenery yet far more wild and uncrowded.

The Border Route Trail is 65 miles long and connects the Superior Hiking Trail with the Kekekabic Trail, cutting across the far eastern part of the BWCA Wilderness. It was planned and built by members of the Minnesota Rovers outdoor club of the Twin Cities. Two other hikes on the Border Route Trail are Bryce Breon Trail (Hike #43) and Magnetic Rock (Hike #44). For info, visit **www.borderroutetrail.org**.

48 Mount Josephine

A 2.5 mile out-and-back hike on the Grand Portage Reservation

From the top of Mount Josephine, the most expansive view of all is toward Pigeon Point, the Susie Islands, and distant Isle Royale.

▶ **What makes it unique.** This rough and challenging trail has the steepest climb—and the most dramatic view—on the North Shore.

▶ **Finding the trailhead.** Follow Highway 61 for 35 miles past Grand Marais to mile marker 144.0, the main turn-off for Grand Portage. Turn right on County Road 17 (you will stay on County Road 17 to the trailhead). Turn left at the four way stop. Follow Mile Creek Road 0.9 miles, past the Grand Portage National Monument information center. Turn left on Upper Road (still County Road 17). Follow Upper Road 0.9 miles to parking lot on left. Watch for fire number 183.

Miigwech (thank you) to the Grand Portage Band of Lake Superior Chippewa for taking care of this beautiful land and making it available for all people to enjoy.

No pain, no gain is a good mantra to adopt for this hike. The terrain requires hard work. Finding the trail and following it is hard work. Fair warning: this trail is not as well maintained as other trails in the area. But the view from the top is extraordinary as you stand at the highest point directly on the Minnesota North Shore.

Once you're parked at the nearly unmarked trailhead, you'll see two rough

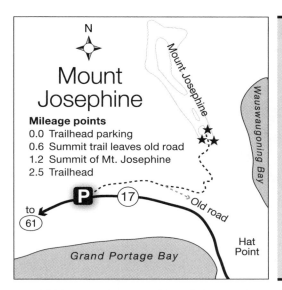

Mount
Josephine

N

Mileage points
0.0 Trailhead parking
0.6 Summit trail leaves old road
1.2 Summit of Mt. Josephine
2.5 Trailhead

to
61

P 17

Old road

Mount Josephine

Wauswaugoning Bay

Hat Point

Grand Portage Bay

Distance: 2.5 miles

Time: 1.5 to 2 hours

Difficulty: difficult. Best for experienced hikers with stamina and the ability to route-find on unmaintained trails. The trail climbs 600 feet in just over a half mile—perhaps the steepest climb on the North Shore.

More info:
McKenzie Map 98: Grand Portage

GPS coordinates:
N47° 58.24'
W089° 40.10'

Trailhead facilities: None

old roads leaving the parking lot. Take the one on the right. The route follows an old, level roadbed.

Watch for the obvious turn off at about 0.6 miles. A sign reads "Summit 1 Mile," and the route heads uphill to the left. It's a remarkably straight traverse, with a climb about one-quarter mile long. Two switchbacks get you to a saddle in an older hardwood forest. Deadfalls across the trail may not have been cleared, so get used to following a beaten path around them.

The last part of the trail is the rocky and steep climb to the summit. The views open gradually and remind you of why you've worked so hard to get here. On top, there are a series of viewpoints looking inland, toward Grand Portage Bay, and toward Hat Point. The biggest view of all is toward Pigeon Point, the Susie Islands, and distant Isle Royale.

This peak is 700 feet higher than Lake Superior below. At 1,300 feet above sea level, Mount Josephine is not as high as Carlton Peak (1,530 feet), but it's much

Nearby Eats, Treats & Lodging

Grand Portage is full of history and culture. Be sure to leave at least an hour to visit the **Grand Portage National Monument** and learn via hands-on exhibits about the fascinating Great Lakes fur trade—the interpretive programs are excellent. The **Grand Portage Lodge and Casino** has comfortable hotel rooms, a pleasant pool, and an RV park for campers.

closer to the lake, so the effect is really breathtaking. A solid stone foundation marks the site of a fire lookout tower. It's a thigh-rumbling hike back down the way you came. There is no water along the hike, so bring plenty on warm summer days.

Views from the Mount Josephine trail summit are stunning. This photo looks north up the shore, toward Canada.

History of Grand Portage

The river town Stillwater claims to be "the birthplace of Minnesota." But the history of Grand Portage goes back much farther than Stillwater.

Before there was a Canada or a United States, the **Grand Portage Trail** was the critical link for travel into the interior of North America. Traditional usage by native people predated the fur trade by perhaps 2,000 years. Grand Portage was the epicenter of the North American fur trade in the late 18th century. It was the site of some of the most colorful days of the voyageurs, as furs and trade goods changed hands and cultures mingled from across the continent.

After the North West Company pulled out of Grand Portage in 1803, the community remained a center of Anishinaabe settlement on the North Shore. The Grand Portage reservation was created as part of the 1854 Treaty of La Pointe. **Grand Portage National Monument** was established in 1958. Today Grand Portage is a thriving community of over 500 people, with its own charter school and the busy lodge and casino.

To learn more about Grand Portage history, visit the **Heritage Center** at the national monument or the interpretive center at the state park.

49 Historic Grand Portage

An 8.0 mile out-and-back hike in Grand Portage National Monument

The Grand Portage trail crosses Poplar Creek near this hike's turnaround point.

▶ **What makes it unique.** While not the most scenic or challenging hike, the Grand Portage trail really makes history come alive.

▶ **Finding the trailhead.** At mile marker 144.0 on Highway 61, turn south at main signed entrance for park and casino. After 100 yards, turn left at intersection onto Mile Creek Road, following signage for the National Monument. Take Mile Creek Road 0.7 miles to Heritage Center parking on left.

There is nothing like this hike anywhere else on the North Shore. Although the hiking itself is pretty basic, there is so much history here and it is so well interpreted that the whole experience comes alive.

The original prehistoric users of the trail likely found their way through some obvious breaks in the rugged terrain. Today's trail follows the same route; it was designed for transportation, not for scenery.

Massive dikes of erosion-resistant diabase cut through the ancient sedimentary rock here. These dikes not only formed most of the falls of the Pigeon River, but also formed the steep terrain for those trying to hike around those falls.

This hike starts at the parking lot for the Heritage Center. The Heritage

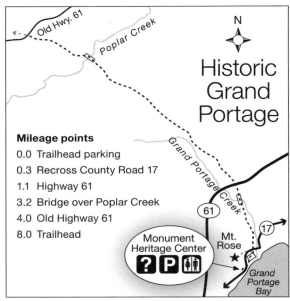

Historic Grand Portage

Mileage points

0.0 Trailhead parking
0.3 Recross County Road 17
1.1 Highway 61
3.2 Bridge over Poplar Creek
4.0 Old Highway 61
8.0 Trailhead

Distance: 8.0 miles

Time: 2.5 to 4 hours

Difficulty: moderate. The trail is wide, well-marked and well-maintained. It climbs almost 500 feet.

More info:
Grand Portage National Monument
(218) 475-0123
www.nps.gov/grpo
Map at Park Service office or McKenzie Map 98: Grand Portage

GPS coordinates:
N47° 57.62'
W089° 41.20'

Trailhead facilities:
Restrooms, drinking water, interpretive exhibits.

Center is highly recommended; the exhibits are excellent, and prepare you well for the hike. There are artifacts that were found on the actual trail on display, as well as a cool 3-D map of the trail and the rugged terrain through which it passes.

Follow the main trail right through the stockade area, including the birch bark structures of the Ojibwe village and the main stockade itself. On the east side of the stockade, you'll pass a trail junction for the Mount Rose trail. Once the route recrosses County Road 17, you'll be on the Grand Portage itself.

The trail is wide and well-maintained. Solid wooden bridges cross creeks such as Grand Portage Creek. It's boreal forest, with balsam fir and birch trees. About a mile in, the trail crosses Highway 61, where there's a great view. There aren't many big open views from the trail, so enjoy this one.

Watch for occasional views of the surrounding terrain through the aspen and birch trees. This is a very different hike in late fall, when the leaves are off the trees and you can see through to the dramatic terrain.

After climbing for the first one and a half miles, the trail flattens out. The forest changes as well, with an ash tree swamp and a 200-yard boardwalk through a beautiful grove of big white pine and balsam fir trees.

As you hike along, try to imagine carrying a ninety-pound pack of trade goods on your back, with only a leather strap around your forehead. Even better, imagine carrying three of those packs. The voyageurs carried multiple packs and did the Grand Portage in stages, carrying part of their load a half mile in, dropping it and returning for another few packs. Look for possible rest stops (called "posés" by the French-Canadian voyageurs) every half mile or so. Here's a hint from recent archeological research: the voyageurs stopped for refreshment, not the views.

If you should be so lucky as to find an historic artifact, you should leave it in its place and take a picture of it; then notify the park office. This is a National Park, and everything here belongs to all of us.

At mile 3, the trail crosses Poplar Creek. Poplar is another name for the aspen, a favored food of the beaver; a large beaver dam stands to the west of the footbridge. After crossing Poplar Creek, a steep trail rolls through a forest of mature aspen trees before it reaches Old Highway 61.

This is your turnaround spot. Enjoy the walk back down to the lake.

▶ **Other options for this hike.** This is an excellent 4.0 mile hike with vehicle shuttle. From Old Highway 61, about ten miles by car on rougher roads, you can hike downhill. This way, you capture the spirit of the voyageurs, who arrived at Grand Portage after a thousand-mile canoe journey. To reach the Old Highway 61 trailhead for a one-way hike, return west on Highway 61 for 0.6 miles to County Road 17 (Mineral Center Road). Take this 4.1 miles to the intersection with County Road 89 (Old Highway 61). Follow Old Highway 61 for 5.0 miles, past turnoffs for Mt. Maud and Partridge Falls. The Grand Portage is marked by signs on both sides of the old paved road.

Rugged hills surround the trading post at Grand Portage National Monument.

Two Grand Portages

Names are already confusing around Grand Portage, where there is a state park, a national monument, a casino and an actual trail all with the same name, "Grand Portage." It gets even more confusing when you throw in another trail off the North Shore with the same name.

Just off the west edge of Duluth, you'll find the Grand Portage of the St. Louis River. The portage passed miles of treacherous rapids to access inland waterways that reached up the St. Louis to the Mississippi River. Just as the Grand Portage of the Pi-

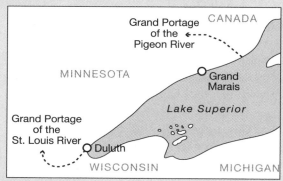

geon River, this portage was the busy route of the voyageurs and explorers during the fur trade area. Records from the Jesuits show the route existed as early as 1670. The portage was seven miles long, two miles shorter than the Grand Portage of the Pigeon River.

Hikers can still follow the two miles or so of the Grand Portage of the St. Louis River in the far eastern area of Jay Cooke State Park, along the Grand Portage and Oak trails.

Explore Grand Portage State Park

Big things can come in small packages. Minnesota's biggest waterfall is in the North Shore's smallest park. Grand Portage packs in enough experiences for at least a half-day of your North Shore vacation. Take in the thundering cascade of the High Falls of the Pigeon River. Then enjoy the new visitor center with its exhibits about the Grand Portage community.

After exploring the park, eat your lunch down at the pretty riverside picnic area.

Grand Portage State Park is a unique partnership between the Minnesota Department of Natural Resources and the Grand Portage Band of Lake Superior Chippewa. It's the only Minnesota state park where the State doesn't actually own the land; here, the Bureau of Indian Affairs owns the land in trust for the Band. The park is also the newest state park on the North Shore, created in 1989.

50 Middle Falls Trail

A 5.1 mile loop hike in Grand Portage State Park, near Grand Portage

At Middle Falls, the Pigeon River roars over a ledge of diabase rock.

> **What makes it unique.** Skirting the Canadian border, this trail leads to Minnesota's highest waterfall as well as its lovely little upstream sister, in a remote and very scenic part of the North Shore.

> **Finding the trailhead.** At the very end of Minnesota Highway 61, just before the Pigeon River border crossing, turn north at park entrance at mile marker 150.8.

The Minnesota North Shore ends here. And it's a fitting conclusion, with a little bit of everything that makes North Shore hiking so great. There are waterfalls, great views, and a bit of physical challenge. There are two spurs off the trail, and both are mandatory, the first to experience the High Falls and the second to take in the best view of the hike.

Stop in at the visitor center and learn more about the region. The trail starts out the back door. If the center is closed, you can pick up the trail by walking around the visitor center to the right. The route starts on the wide, paved half-mile trail to the High Falls. This is a popular trail for all ages. Interpretive signs focus on "Nookomis," an Anishinaabe grandmother, and the Anishinaabe's seasonal gatherings from the woods. There are comfy benches all along the paved trail, making it a very easy hike for kids or the elderly.

Distance: 5.1 miles

Time: 2 to 3 hours

Difficulty: moderate. The first half mile to High Falls is on wide, paved trail. After that, the trail gets narrow and steep, climbing almost 400 feet.

More info:
Grand Portage State Park (218) 475-2360
www.dnr.state.
mn.us/state_parks/
grand_portage
Map at park office

GPS coordinates:
N 48° 00.00'
W 089° 35.55'

Trailhead facilities: Restrooms, drinking water, picnic area.

Mileage points

0.0 Trailhead parking
0.5 High Falls viewing platforms
1.4 Junction to scenic overlooks
2.2 Start of loop
2.8 Middle Falls
3.1 End of loop
5.1 Trailhead

For a change of scenery, take the side trail that goes down steps at about mile 0.2. For about 200 yards this side trail runs along the riverbank, parallel to the main trail. Here the Pigeon River is wide and runs in many smaller channels. Before returning to the main trail, you'll see where the Pigeon emerges from a canyon into the open channel. Note the stacks of sedimentary rock on the far (Canadian) side of the river.

The trail to High Falls is the park's Hiking Club Trail, and you will find the password up near the Falls.

The viewing platforms for the High Falls make a great final destination for casual hikers. This is the highest waterfall in Minnesota, and you can watch it plunge over a wall of harder igneous rock into a narrow gorge of easily eroded sedimentary rock. Some days, there's enough mist coming off the falls to make a rainbow.

After enjoying the High Falls, return from the viewing platforms to the start of the Middle Falls trail near an outhouse.

The trail, rougher and narrower now, climbs up and over a high ridge. This is part of the same chunk of erosion-resistant diabase that formed the High

Falls. At the top of the ridge, watch for a turn off to the right for a scenic overlook. The spur leads 100 yards along the ridgeline to the scenic highlight of the hike. There are two viewing spots, one on each side of the ridge; be sure to continue to the second. In the distance you see Pigeon Point and Finger Point; the Pigeon River runs through the valley below.

After the ridge, the trail descends steeply and passes through young balsam fir trees. The climax of the hike is the one-mile loop to Middle Falls. At the loop junction, turn right and do the loop counter-clockwise. That way you approach Middle Falls from below, a more dramatic approach.

Water pours through many channels over the High Falls (top); the view from the second spur takes in the Pigeon River valley and distant Finger Point (middle); spring flowers, like bloodroot, line the upper trail (bottom).

The first view is from across a large pool.

Middle Falls is a substantial waterfall, well worth the trek for the devoted waterfall fan. You can get quite close to the Falls as you continue around the loop. Canada is literally a stone's throw away across the current. After visiting Middle Falls, finish the loop and return the way you came. Save some energy for the return hike: it's a steep climb back up and over the ridge.

Resources and contacts for hikers

Trail organizations

Please consider supporting these North Shore volunteer and nonprofit organizations with a donation of time or money.

- Superior Hiking Trail Association, (218) 834-2700 | www.superiorhiking.org
- Border Route Trail Association | www.borderroutetrail.org
- Kekekabic Trail Club | northcountrytrail.org/trail/minnesota/kek

Shuttle services

- The Superior Hiking Shuttle, Fridays through Sundays, May through October, plus year-round specialized service. www.superiorhikingshuttle.com or 218-834-5511.
- Harriet Quarles Transportation, spring through fall, www.harrietquarles.com or 866-387-1801 or (email) harrietq@boreal.org.

Federal agencies

The national forests and national parks are the backbone of our American identity—and both are found here on the North Shore.

- Superior National Forest, (218) 626-4300 | www.fs.usda.gov/superior
- Superior National Forest Tofte District, (218) 663-8060 | tofte@fs.fed.us
- Superior National Forest Gunflint District, (218) 387-1750 | gunflint@fs.fed.us
- Grand Portage National Monument, (218) 475-0123 | www.nps.gov/grpo

State Parks and agencies

North Shore state parks are often called "the crown jewels" of Minnesota's extensive park system.

- Jay Cooke State Park, (218) 673-7000
  www.dnr.state.mn.us/state_parks/jay_cooke
- Gooseberry Falls State Park, (218) 595-7100
  www.dnr.state.mn.us/state_parks/gooseberry_falls
- Split Rock Lighthouse State Park, (218) 595-7625
  www.dnr.state.mn.us/state_parks/split_rock_lighthouse
- Tettegouche State Park, (218) 353-8800
  www.dnr.state.mn.us/state_parks/Tettegouche

- George H. Crosby Manitou State Park, c/o Tettegouche State Park
  (218) 353-8800 | www.dnr.state.mn.us/state_parks/george_crosby_manitou
- Temperance River State Park, (218) 663-3100
  www.dnr.state.mn.us/state_parks/temperance_river
- Cascade River State Park, (218) 387-6000
  www.dnr.state.mn.us/state_parks/cascade_river
- Judge C.R. Magney State Park, (218) 387-6300
  www.dnr.state.mn.us/state_parks/judge_cr_magney
- Grand Portage State Park, (218) 475-2360
  www.dnr.state.mn.us/state_parks/grand_portage
- Scientific and Natural Areas
  www.dnr.state.mn.us/snas

Recommended reading
Guidebooks

- *The Hiker's BWCA Wilderness Companion: Kekekabic Trail Guide*, Angela Anderson (1996, Kekekabic Trail Club, Roseville)
- *50 Circuit Hikes: A Stride-by-Stride Guide to Northeastern Minnesota*, Howard Fenton (2002, University of Minnesota Press, Minneapolis)
- *Gooseberry Falls to Grand Portage*, Ron Morton and Steve Morse (2007, Rockflower Press, Knife River)
- *A Walking Guide to the Superior Hiking Trail*, Ron Morton and Judy Gibbs (2006, Rockflower Press, Knife River)
- *Hiking Minnesota II*, Mary Jo Mosher and Kristine Mosher (2002, Falcon Press, Helena)
- *Hiking Minnesota*, John Pukite (1998, Falcon Press, Helena)
- *The Border Route Trail: A Trail Guide and Map*, Marcia Scott and Chuck Hoffman (2012, Border Route Trail Association, Edina)
- *Camping the North Shore, 2nd Edition: A guide to the best campgrounds in Minnesota's spectacular Lake Superior region*, Andrew Slade (2019, There and Back Books, Duluth)
- *Skiing the North Shore: A guide to cross country trails in Minnesota's spectacular Lake Superior region*, Andrew Slade (2007, There and Back Books, Duluth)
- *Guide to the Superior Hiking Trail*, Eighth Edition, Superior Hiking Trail Association (2017, Superior Hiking Trail Association, Two Harbors)
- *Waterfalls of Minnesota's North Shore*, Eve and Gary Wallinga (2006, North Shore Press, Hovland)

Natural History

- *The North Shore Birding Trail: A Guide to Birding Minnesota's North Shore of Lake Superior from Duluth to Grand Portage*, Audubon Minnesota (2007, National Audubon Society, New York City)
- *Geology on Display: Geology and Scenery of Minnesota's North Shore State Parks*, John C. Green (1996, State of Minnesota, St. Paul)
- *Gunflint Burning: Fire in the Boundary Waters*, Cary J. Griffith (2018, University of Minnesota Press, Minneapolis)
- *Fascinating Fungi of the North Woods*, Cora Mollen and Larry Weber (2006, Kollath-Stensaas Publishing, Duluth)
- *Wildflowers of the BWCA and North Shore*, Mark Stensaas (2003, Kollath-Stensaas Publishing, Duluth)
- *The Superior North Shore*, Thomas Waters (1999, University of Minnesota Press, Minneapolis)

Index

About the author

photo: © Rolf Hagberg Photography

Andrew Slade's parents first set eyes on each other on the North Shore, and his life has centered there since birth—despite growing up in the Twin Cities. As a kid, he caught nets full of smelt at the Cross River, jumped cliffs into the deep pools of an unnamed North Shore river, helped to band woodcock in the open fields of North Shore homesteads, and shut his eyes tight each time the family wagon drove around Silver Cliff (readers, don't worry— today there's a tunnel through the cliff and his eyes stay wide open). With his intrepid father, he had to abandon a mid-1970s assault on Carlton Peak due to a lack of recognizable trails.

As a canoe guide and outdoor educator in Ely, he learned that "sauna" is a three-syllable word (sow-ooh-nah). In his twenties, he bushwhacked by snowshoe much of what is now the Manitou-Caribou section of the Superior Hiking Trail. At age 28, in his "before kids" era, he was the editor and lead author of the first *Guide to the Superior Hiking Trail*.

Slade graduated from the University of Minnesota with a BA in environmental education and from the University of Montana with a MS in environmental studies. His favorite wildflower is *Mertensia paniculata*, the native North Shore bluebell.

Andrew has worked for environmental education, parks and conservation organizations on the North Shore since 1992. Reach him at **andrewhslade@gmail.com**.

About There and Back Books. We live and play in northern Minnesota—a fabulous landscape filled with wild rivers, deep woods, diverse wildlife, and the greatest Lake. An abundance of great trails, campgrounds, state parks, outfitters, and lodging makes this landscape accessible to nearly everyone. Our guidebooks feature detailed maps, dozens of photographs, and descriptive text to boost your confidence and get you safely "out there"...and back. We'll see you on the trail!

THERE AND BACK BOOKS READ. GO. DISCOVER.
www.bestnorthshore.com
Your guide to Minnesota's spectacular Lake Superior region